YOUR RIGHTS

to money benefits 2008/09

Age Concern's bestselling guide

Sally West

Age Concern England would like to thank the Department for Work and Pensions for its comments on the text. The author also thanks Sheelagh Donovan, Fran Gonsalves, Ben Moore, Anna Nalecz and Michael Roche from Age Concern England's Information Unit for their contributions.

Published by Age Concern England
1268 London Road
London SW16 4ER

© 2008 Age Concern England

Thirty-sixth Edition

This edition prepared by Sally West

Editor Ro Lyon
Production Keith Hawkins

Typeset by GreenGate Publishing Services, Tonbridge, Kent

Printed in Great Britain by Bell & Bain Ltd, Glasgow

A catalogue record for this book is available from the British Library.

ISBN-13: 978 0 86242 432 9

We hope that this publication has been useful to you. If so, we would very much like to hear from you. Alternatively, if you feel that we could add or change anything, then please write and tell us, using the following Freepost Address: Age Concern, FREEPOST CN1794, LONDON SW16 4BR.

Contents

Introduction

This book provides information about the main financial benefits and entitlements available for older people. Most of the information applies to those aged 60 and over. The benefit rates given generally apply from the week beginning 7 April 2008.

Your Rights is divided into five parts. The first section gives details about pensions and retirement, and the second section is about financial help for those on low incomes. The third part covers benefits and financial support for disabled people and their carers, including the system of help towards paying for care, while the fourth gives information about other types of financial help.

Many of the subjects covered in *Your Rights* can be complicated, and the book aims to explain them as simply as possible. However, it cannot cover all situations and circumstances. If you need more information, the fifth section gives details about obtaining relevant leaflets from the Department for Work and Pensions (DWP – formerly called the Department of Social Security), Age Concern information and contacting other local and national sources of help. There is also an index and a summary of the main benefit rates on pages 212–213.

The State pensions and benefits described in this book are delivered through DWP agencies: The Pension Service, the Disability and Carers Service (which have now been merged into a single agency) and Jobcentre

Plus. There is more information about this and how to contact the relevant office on page 198. Older people will mainly deal with The Pension Service – either through one of the regional pension centres or the local Pension Service.

Please note that although some older people have young families, benefits for children are not covered in this book. People with dependent children or who are under the age of 60 should contact a local advice agency or Jobcentre Plus office for information about benefit entitlements.

Where you live in the United Kingdom

All the information covered in *Your Rights* applies to people living in England. It also applies to Scotland and Wales except where differences are pointed out in the text. Although there is a separate social security system in Northern Ireland, the social security benefits available are generally the same. However, there may be some differences in the sources of financial help discussed in Part 4 'Other Benefits and Financial Support' and local and national sources of further information will also be different.

For further information or advice relating to older people living in Scotland, contact the Scottish Helpline for Older People on 0845 125 9732; for Wales and Northern Ireland, contact Age Concern Cymru or Age Concern Northern Ireland – the addresses are on page 222.

If you are living in the UK but subject to immigration control, your benefit position may be affected. This book does not provide information about immigration status, so contact a local advice agency if you need further details.

Living abroad

Many of the benefits covered in this book will not apply to you if you are living abroad permanently, or they may stop during a temporary stay abroad. In some cases there are special rules for people who live in the European Economic Area (EEA). The EEA is made up of all the European Union countries plus Iceland, Liechtenstein and Norway. The same rules also apply to Switzerland, even though it is not a member of the EEA. Gibraltar is treated as a separate state for social security purposes.

As this book does not give full details about the benefit postion for people living abroad, for more information contact your pension centre (if you are currently in this country) or the International Pension Centre, The Pension Service, Tyneview Park, Whitley Road, Benton, Newcastle upon Tyne NE98 1BA, Tel: 0191 218 7777; this is the part of the DWP that deals with pensions and benefits paid abroad.

Keeping up to date

This book is based on information available in the middle of March 2008. If you would like to be kept up to date with any changes during the year, you can fill in the form on page 214.

If you need more information about any of the issues covered in the book, please write to Age Concern England at the address on page 222. A new edition of *Your Rights* will be available in April 2009 – please let us know if you have any comments or suggestions.

Pensions

This part of *Your Rights* contains information about the State Pension. There is also a section which describes what is available to people before and after State Pension age. In addition there are details about the Christmas Bonus (paid to people receiving a State Pension or certain other benefits); the procedure for appealing against a social security decision; and occupational and personal pensions.

STATE PENSIONS

The State Pension is paid to people who have reached State Pension age (currently 60 for women born on or before 5 April 1950, 65 for men) and who fulfil the National Insurance (NI) contribution conditions. The amount you receive is not affected by your income and savings but it is taxable.

You can draw your State Pension even if you are still working. Alternatively, you can choose not to draw your State Pension at State Pension age and instead receive extra State Pension or a one-off taxable lump-sum payment at a later date.

Your State Pension may consist of a Basic State Pension plus an Additional State Pension (based on contributions after April 1978) and a Graduated Retirement Benefit (based on contributions between April 1961 and April 1975). You will receive an extra 25p each week when you reach the age of 80. These different parts of the State Pension are explained below. Whether you are entitled to a State Pension or not, you may be able to claim other benefits, such as Pension Credit, Housing Benefit and Council Tax Benefit, which depend on your income and savings.

> FOR MORE INFORMATION, *see Pension Service guide NP46* A Guide to State Pensions, *which is only available on the website (www.thepensionservice. gov.uk).*

Changes to State Pension age

By 2020 State Pension age will be 65 for both men and women. The increase in the age for women will be phased in over ten years starting in 2010. State Pension age for women born on or before 5 April 1950 will remain at 60. State Pension age for women born on or after 6 April 1950 and on or before 5 April 1955 will be between 60 years and 1 month and 64 years and 11 months, depending on the exact date of birth. (For more information, see the table in Pension Service guide NP46). For women born on or after 6 April 1955, State Pension age will be 65.

As a result of changes introduced by *The Pensions Act 2007*, State Pension age will gradually increase to 68 for both men and women in three stages between 2024 and 2046. This will affect anyone born after 5 April 1959.

Civil partnerships

Since December 2005 same-sex couples have been able to form a civil partnership. State Pension provisions that previously applied to both husbands and wives now also apply to registered civil partners. However, where provisions apply only to women, such as the married women's pension, rules will only be extended to civil partners when State Pension age starts to be equalised for men and women in 2010 (when they will also apply to married men).

Future changes to State Pensions

As a result of changes introduced by *The Pensions Act 2007*, contribution conditions for State Pensions will change, affecting people reaching State Pension age on or after 6 April 2010. From this date people will be able to get the full Basic State Pension if they have 30 years of contributions and/or credits. There will also be a new carer credit which will replace the current system of Home Responsibilities Protection for those caring for a

3

sick or disabled person or a child up to the age of 12 and foster carers. People will no longer need to have paid contributions for a minimum number of years to receive any Basic State Pension. Also, the annual increase in the Basic State Pension will, from 2012 (or slightly later), be linked to changes in average earnings instead of prices. There will be more information in future editions of *Your Rights*.

> FOR MORE INFORMATION *about changes to State Pensions, see the Pensions Reform section of the DWP website (www.dwp.gov.uk/pensionsreform). Contact The Pension Service if you need information about your own pension position.*

BASIC STATE PENSION

The Basic State Pension is paid at the same rate to everyone who has fulfilled the NI contribution conditions. The full weekly rates are shown as follows:

Single person	£90.70
Wife on husband's contributions	£54.35
Married couple on husband's contributions	£145.05
Couple	£181.40

(if both have full contribution records)

You may hear the terms 'Category A' and 'Category B' pensions. Category A State Pensions are generally based on an individual's own contributions, while Category B State Pensions are based on a spouse or civil partner's record – for example the State Pension paid to married women or a widow/er or bereaved civil partner. Both types of State Pension consist of a Basic and/or Additional State Pension.

Who qualifies?

You will receive the full Basic State Pension if you have paid NI contributions at the appropriate rate for most of the years of your working life, or if any gaps in your record are covered by credits or Home Responsibilities Protection, as explained later. If you have not paid enough, you may get a reduced State Pension or you may not get a State Pension at all (see 'Your contributions', pages 11–15).

Normally you need to have satisfied the contribution conditions in your own right; but married women, divorcees, widowed people, and those whose civil partnership has ended through bereavement or dissolution, may be able to claim a State Pension on their spouse/partner's or former spouse/partner's contributions, as explained in the following pages.

Pensions for married women

If you are a married woman and you have paid appropriate contributions for most of your working life, you should be entitled to the Basic State Pension of £90.70 a week. You may also get a full Basic State Pension if you have at least one year of paid contributions with the remaining record made up of credits. If you have paid full contributions and/or received credits for only part of your working life, you may be entitled to a reduced State Pension. However, any years when you were paying the married woman's reduced-rate contributions will not count towards a State Pension.

If you are 60 or over but do not have enough paid contributions and credits for a State Pension in your own right, you cannot get any Basic State Pension until your husband draws his. When your husband draws his State Pension, you should claim the married woman's State Pension, which will be £54.35 a week if your husband has a full contribution record.

If at the age of 60 you are entitled to a Basic State Pension on your own contributions of less than £54.35 a week, it can be made up to a maximum of £54.35 a week when your husband draws his State Pension. Following changes to the rules, due to be in place by April 2008, if you are already receiving a State Pension on your own contributions when your husband claims his, The Pension Service will do this automatically. You will still need to make a claim if you are not already getting your State Pension at the time of your husband's claim. However, if your own Basic State Pension is more than £54.35 a week, you cannot get any extra State Pension based on your husband's contributions. On top of any Basic State Pension you receive, you may also be entitled to Graduated Retirement Benefit and/or Additional State Pension based on any contributions you have made, as explained on pages 21–22 and 28–29.

Sometimes married women who have paid NI contributions in the past but who are not working when they reach 60, do not realise that they may be entitled to some State Pension based on their earlier contributions. The State Pension is not awarded automatically – you have to make a claim. So if you think you may be entitled to a State Pension, and you have not been contacted about making a claim, contact The Pension Service. However, you should be aware that if you are already receiving a State Pension or another benefit, such as a State Pension based on your husband's contributions or a Widow's Pension, you may not be entitled to anything more.

Future changes to married women's pensions From 6
April 2010, you will be able to claim the married
woman's pension provided your husband has reached his
State Pension age, even if he decides to defer claiming
his own State Pension (see pages 29–35). Married men
and civil partners may also be entitled to a State Pension
or an increase to their own State Pension based on their
spouse's or civil partner's contributions, provided their
spouse or civil partner was born on or after 6 April 1950
and has reached State Pension age.

Increases for dependants

Dependent wives If you are under 60 when your
husband draws his State Pension (at 65 or over), and you
live together, he may be able to claim for you as a
dependant, and his State Pension will be increased by a
maximum of £54.35 a week. However, your husband
will not receive any increase for you if you receive
certain State benefits of £54.35 a week or more. The
increase may also be affected by any earnings you have.
He will not be able to receive the increase if you are
working and earn more than £60.50 a week (after certain
expenses connected with work have been deducted). Any
occupational or personal pension you receive will be
counted as earnings.

If you do not live with your husband, he may be able to
receive an increase if he is making a contribution to your
maintenance. He will not be able to receive this increase
if you receive certain State benefits of £54.35 a week or
more, or if you earn more than £54.35 a week.

Dependent husbands If you are a married man and
your wife is receiving a State Pension, she may be able
to get an increase for you of up to £54.35 a week,

7

provided you are not earning more than £60.50 a week (£54.35 if you do not live with your wife). However, she can get this increase only if she is receiving Incapacity Benefit with an addition for you immediately before she starts to draw the State Pension. Your wife will not receive any increase if you have a State Pension or certain other benefits of £54.35 or more.

Future changes to increases for dependants From 6 April 2010, you will no longer be able to make a claim for an increase for a dependant. This also applies if you reach State Pension age before then but you defer claiming your State Pension until that date or later. There will be some transitional protection for existing claims at 6 April 2010.

Divorce, dissolved civil partnerships and separation

Divorced people If you are divorced but do not qualify for a full State Pension based on your own contributions, you may be able to use your former spouse's contribution record to increase the amount of Basic State Pension you receive to the maximum pension for a single person of £90.70 a week. You are not entitled to your former spouse's Graduated Retirement Benefit or Additional State Pension. (However, since December 2000, when rules on 'pension sharing' came into effect, it has been possible for Additional State Pension to be divided as part of a divorce settlement.)

Your former spouse's contribution record is substituted for your own from the start of your working life up until your divorce or just for the period of your marriage.

If you get divorced before State Pension age, you may need to pay further contributions after your divorce to qualify for a Basic State Pension. If you are a woman who gets divorced after State Pension age and are receiving the married woman's State Pension, you may be able to use the rules outlined above to get a full State Pension. If you remarry or form a civil partnership before State Pension age, you cannot claim a State Pension on your former husband's or wife's contributions. However, if you remarry or form a civil partnership after State Pension age, you will not lose any State Pension based on your previous spouse's contributions.

Dissolved civil partnerships The term 'dissolution' is used if civil partners legally separate and is the equivalent of divorce for married couples. Pension rules will be the same as those described here for divorced people.

Separated women If you are separated from your husband and do not qualify for a Basic State Pension on your own contributions when you reach 60, or you are only entitled to a State Pension of less than £54.35 a week, you may be able to claim the married woman's State Pension of up to £54.35 a week when your husband claims his.

State Pensions for widows and widowers and surviving civil partners

This section looks at the amount of State Pension that a widow, widower or surviving civil partner can receive at State Pension age. For information about benefits for people bereaved under State Pension age, see pages 160–163.

Widows If you were under 60 when your husband died and you have not remarried or formed a civil partnership, you may be entitled to the State Pension based on your late husband's contributions and/or your own, once you reach State Pension age. The amount you receive will depend upon your own, and your late husband's, contribution record and the age at which you were widowed. If you were 60 or over when your husband died, and not receiving the full Basic State Pension, you may be able to use his contribution record to bring your Basic State Pension up to a maximum of £90.70 a week.

You may also receive Additional State Pension and/or Graduated Retirement Benefit based on your husband's contributions, as explained on pages 26–28 and 29.

Once you are drawing the State Pension at age 60 or over, you can remarry, form a civil partnership or live with a partner without losing a State Pension based on your previous husband's contributions.

Widowers and surviving civil partners If you were bereaved on or after 6 April 1979 and do not have enough contributions of your own, you may be entitled to a State Pension based on your wife's or civil partner's contributions, provided you were both over State Pension age when they died. You may also inherit some of your wife/civil partner's Additional State Pension and/or Graduated Retirement Benefit, as explained on pages 27–28 and 29.

If you do not fulfil the above conditions, perhaps because you were bereaved before State Pension age, once you reach State Pension age you may in some circumstances be able to use your wife/civil partner's contribution record in order to increase your Basic State Pension up to a maximum of £90.70 a week. You may also receive Additional State Pension based on your wife/civil partner's contribution record (see pages 27–28).

10

Once you are receiving a State Pension at age 65 or over, you will not lose any State Pension based on your former wife/civil partner's contributions if you remarry or enter a civil partnership.

Your contributions

This section explains the contribution conditions for the Basic State Pension. Your contribution record will depend on the NI contributions you have paid, any 'credits' you received, and any Home Responsibilities Protection you receive. (However, as explained on pages 3–4, the rules will change for people reaching State Pension age on or after 6 April 2010.)

If you have earnings of £90 a week or more (the level of the 'Lower Earnings Limit' in 2008/09), you will be building up entitlement to the Basic Pension. However, you do not start to pay NI contributions until your earnings reach £105 a week. If you have earnings between £90 and £105, you will be treated as though you are paying NI contributions and will still be building up entitlement to the Basic State Pension and other contributory benefits. When reference is made in this book to people who have 'paid' NI contributions, this includes people with earnings between £90 and £105 a week and who are thus treated as having paid NI contributions.

There are two conditions that you must meet in order to receive a State Pension. The first condition is that you have paid sufficient contributions during at least one year in your working life since 6 April 1975 or paid at least 50 flat-rate contributions at any time before 6 April 1975. Credited contributions cannot count towards this first condition.

11

The second condition is that to receive a full Basic State Pension you must normally have paid or been credited with contributions for 90 per cent of the years of your working life. To receive any Basic State Pension at all you must have a minimum number of years' contributions (normally 10 for a woman or 11 for a man).

Whether you will get a full Basic State Pension depends on your 'working life' and 'qualifying years', and whether your contribution record has been protected by credits and/or Home Responsibilities Protection. These terms are explained below.

If you are more than 30 days away from State Pension age it is normally possible to get a forecast to check whether you have paid enough contributions to get a full State Pension. At the time of writing, the systems are being updated to take into account the changes that are being introduced. So forecasts can only be made for those reaching State Pension age on or before 5 April 2010. The full service should be running by Autumn 2008.

TO APPLY FOR A STATE PENSION FORECAST, complete form BR19, which is obtainable from The Pension Service by ringing 0845 300 0168 or using the online service on the website (www.thepensionservice. gov.uk).

Both men and women aged 80 or over who have not paid enough contributions for a Basic State Pension might qualify for the non-contributory State Pension described on pages 35–36.

How are contributions paid? Since April 1975 employed people have paid contributions as a percentage of earnings, and these are collected with Income Tax. Self-employed people pay flat-rate contributions each

week which count towards the Basic State Pension. If
your taxable income is over a certain amount, extra
contributions will be collected with your Income Tax.

Which contributions count? If you paid the married
woman's or widow's reduced-rate contributions, these do
not count towards a State Pension in your own right.
Contributions made abroad may help you qualify for the
Basic State Pension if you worked in another European
Union country or one which has a reciprocal agreement
with the UK.

Working life Your 'working life' is the period on which
your contribution record is based. This normally starts in
the tax year (ie 6 April to 5 April) when you were 16
and ends with the last full tax year before you reach
State Pension age (currently 60 for women born on or
before 5 April 1950, 65 for men). A woman reaching
State Pension age now has a working life of 44 years
and a man reaching State Pension age now has a
working life of 49 years.

Qualifying years A 'qualifying year' is a tax year in
which you have paid or been credited with enough
contributions to go towards a State Pension. Since 1978 a
'qualifying year' has been one in which contributions are
paid on earnings which are the same as, or more than, 52
times the weekly Lower Earnings Limit. (Between April
1975 and April 1978 the qualifying earnings were 50
times the Lower Earnings Limit.) This tax year, 2008/09,
the Lower Earnings Limit is £90 a week.

Before 1975 working people paid contributions by
weekly stamp. To work out your qualifying years before
1975, all your stamps (paid and credited) are added up
and divided by 50, rounding up any that are left over –

13

but you cannot have more qualifying years worked out in this way than the number of years in your working life up to April 1975.

Credits If you are under State Pension age (currently 60 for women born on or before 5 April 1950, 65 for men), you may receive a credit in place of a National Insurance contribution in certain circumstances. For example, you will receive a credit for each week you register for Jobseeker's Allowance and are seeking work or you are unable to work because you are sick or disabled or you are receiving Carer's Allowance. Men aged 60–64 who are not paying contributions will normally receive credits automatically even if they are not ill or signing on as unemployed. However, men cannot get these automatic credits for any tax year during which they are abroad for more than six months. They will be gradually phased out for men who reach age 60 after 5 October 2010.

Late and voluntary contributions If there are periods when you will not be paying contributions, perhaps because you will be abroad, you may want to consider paying voluntary contributions to protect your State Pension record. If there are gaps in your contribution record, it is sometimes possible to pay late contributions. But note that for people reaching State Pension age on or after 6 April 2010 the rules are changing so that you will need fewer years of contributions to receive a full State Pension (see pages 3–4). So get advice if you are not sure whether you will benefit from paying voluntary contributions.

Voluntary contributions must normally be paid by the end of the sixth tax year after the one in which they are due. After the tax year has ended people are usually contacted if they have gaps in their contribution record and invited to pay voluntary contributions. However, these letters were not sent out for the years 1996/97 to 2000/01, so there are special rules that extend the time limits for paying backdated contributions for these years. People who may have missed out should have been contacted about this but if you need more information contact The Pension Service, HM Revenue & Customs (HMRC – previously the Inland Revenue) or a local advice agency.

Calculating your pension

If you will reach State Pension age on or before 5 April 2010, in order to be entitled to a full Basic State Pension about nine out of every ten years of your working life have to be qualifying years. This means that women with a working life of 44 years will normally need 39 qualifying years for a full State Pension. Men with a working life of 49 years will normally need 44 qualifying years for a full State Pension.

If you are not entitled to the full Basic State Pension, you may get a reduced one provided you have at least a quarter of the qualifying years you need for a full State Pension.

Example

Christina Paretsky was born on 10 August 1948 and was 16 in 1964. Her working life runs from 6 April 1964 to 5 April 2008, a total of 44 years. To receive a full Basic State Pension, she needs 39 or more qualifying years. She has worked and paid contributions for only 20 years of her working life, and is not entitled to any credits or Home Responsibilities Protection, so she will receive about half the Basic State Pension.

15

Home Responsibilities Protection

Home Responsibilities Protection (HRP) started in 1978 to protect the contribution record of people caring for a child or a sick or disabled person. It helps protect your Basic State Pension and since 6 April 2002 may help you build up Additional State Pension through the State Second Pension (see page 23).

You cannot get HRP for the years when you were looking after someone before April 1978.

You may receive HRP if you worked and paid full NI contributions for part of the year but not enough to count as a qualifying year. However, a married woman or widow cannot get HRP for any tax year in which she, if she was working, would only be due to pay reduced-rate NI contributions.

You are entitled to HRP if you meet any of the following conditions, or in some situations a combination of them, for a whole tax year (but note that the rules changed for the third condition):

- You get Child Benefit for a child under 16.

- You get Income Support because you are looking after a sick or disabled person and therefore do not need to register for Jobseeker's Allowance.

- For at least 35 hours a week you look after someone who receives, for a minimum of 48 weeks in the year, Attendance Allowance, the middle or highest rate of the care component of Disability Living Allowance, or Constant Attendance Allowance. For tax years before 6 April 1994, the allowance had to be paid for 52 weeks.

- You are a registered foster parent (for years from 2003/04 onwards).

If you get Carer's Allowance, you will normally be getting NI credits towards your State Pension so you will not need HRP, although you cannot get credits or HRP if you retained the right to pay the married woman's reduced-rate contributions.

How to work it out HRP makes it easier for you to qualify for a Basic State Pension. Each year of 'home responsibility' will be taken away from the number of qualifying years you need to get a full Basic State Pension. However, HRP cannot be used to reduce the number of qualifying years to below 20.

Example

Eileen Smith, who was born in 1948, started work at 16 and paid full contributions for 15 years until 1979 when she gave up paid work to look after her children. After 14 years at home, she returned to paid work until she became 60 in 2008. Her State Pension was worked out in the following way:

Working life	44 years
Number of qualifying years needed for a full Basic State Pension	39 years
Number of years of HRP	14 years
Number of qualifying years needed for a full Basic State Pension after taking away years of HRP	25 years

Normally Eileen would need to have paid contributions for 39 years in order to receive a full Basic State Pension. However, because her 14 years of HRP reduce the number of qualifying years she needs to 25, she is entitled to the full Basic State Pension although she has paid only 30 years of contributions.

When to claim HRP should be given automatically if you qualify under the first two conditions described above. You should not have to claim.

You must claim HRP if you qualify under the third or fourth condition – because you are looking after someone who is getting one of the allowances mentioned above, such as Attendance Allowance, or because you are a foster parent – or if you qualify under one condition for part of the tax year and under another for the rest of the year.

Claims for HRP in respect of caring years before 2002/03 can be made at any time up to State Pension age. However, for years from April 2002 onwards you will need to claim by the end of the third year following the year for which you are claiming HRP. For example, for caring during the 2005/06 tax year you should claim between 6 April 2006 and 5 April 2009. Ask for leaflet CF411 from HM Revenue & Customs; it is also available online (at www.hmrc.gov. uk/forms/cf411.pdf).

How to claim your State Pension

About four months before you reach State Pension age you should be sent a claim pack. You can ring 0845 300 1084 to make a claim over the phone or to ask for a claim form. If you have not been contacted about claiming your State Pension three months before your birthday, contact The Pension Service or ring 0845 300 1084. A married woman claiming a State Pension on her husband's contributions will need to make a separate claim.

You may decide not to draw your State Pension at 60 (women) or 65 (men) in order to gain extra State Pension or a lump-sum payment. This is known as 'deferring' your State Pension and is explained on pages 29–35. If you do defer, when you want to start claiming the State Pension, contact The Pension Service well in advance.

How your State Pension is paid

Most people now receive their State Pension paid by Direct Payment into an account. When you apply for your State Pension you will be given information about the different types of bank, building society and post office accounts. You can choose to have your State Pension paid weekly in advance or four-weekly or quarterly in arrears.

If you cannot manage an account or you do not provide account details, you will be sent a weekly cheque in the post. You can sign the back of the cheque to authorise someone else to collect your State Pension at the Post Office. If, for example, you have different carers collecting your State Pension, this may be the best way of getting your money each week. There are also ways of authorising someone else to collect your money from a post office, or bank or building society account.

When you are deciding how to have your State Pension paid, consider the different options – if you are unsure, a local advice agency may be able to help.

FOR MORE INFORMATION, see Age Concern Information Guide Payment of Pensions and Benefits into Bank Accounts, which is available from the Age Concern Information Line on 0800 00 99 66.

Pay-day for anyone who started to draw their State Pension before 28 September 1984 is normally Thursday. For people who retired after that date, pay-day is usually Monday, although if your spouse is already receiving a State Pension on Thursday, you can choose to have yours on the same day. Payments are only made for full weeks and you cannot receive any State Pension for days of retirement before your first pay-day.

Most State Pensions of £5 a week or less are paid once a year, in December, in arrears. If you ask for payment by Direct Payment, you will be paid by that method; otherwise you will be sent a cheque.

Going abroad or living there If you receive your payment by weekly cheque, you must cash this within one month of the date shown on it. If you are going abroad for longer than this (or for a shorter period but do not want the cheques sent while you are away), contact The Pension Service well in advance to discuss how to receive your money when you return. If your pension is paid into an account, you do not need to tell The Pension Service unless you are staying abroad for more than six months.

If you are going abroad for some time, you can, if you wish, arrange to receive your State Pension in the country where you are staying. If you remain abroad, the annual State Pension increase will be paid only if you are living in a European Union country or in a country with which the UK has special arrangements.

FOR MORE INFORMATION, contact your pension centre or the International Pension Centre, The Pension Service, Tyneview Park, Whitley Road, Benton, Newcastle upon Tyne NE98 1BA. Tel: 0191 218 7777.

Going into hospital Before April 2005 your State Pension could be reduced after a period of time in hospital. But the rules were changed, and now your State Pension will continue to be paid however long you are in hospital. If you are receiving benefits such as Attendance Allowance, these may still be affected by a hospital stay.

FOR MORE INFORMATION, see DWP leaflet GIHA5DWP Going into Hospital?

If you disagree with a decision

If you think that you have been awarded the wrong amount of State Pension, or disagree with another decision to do with your State Pension, you can either ask for the decision to be revised or appeal against it. Further details are given on pages 41–45.

ADDITIONAL STATE PENSION

This scheme started on 6 April 1978. From 1978 to April 2002, Additional State Pension was built up under the State Earnings-Related Pension Scheme (SERPS) but since April 2002 the Additional State Pension has been built up under the State Second Pension.

When you receive your State Pension you may receive Additional State Pension on top of your Basic State Pension or you may qualify for an Additional State Pension even if you do not receive any Basic State Pension. The Additional State Pension is taxable.

The Additional State Pension is based on earnings, and on any credited earnings that some carers and long-term sick or disabled people have been entitled to following the introduction of the State Second Pension in April 2002. However, you do not build up any Additional

State Pension based on your earnings if you are self-employed, paying the reduced-rate married woman's contributions, or earning less than the Lower Earnings Limit (which is £90 a week in 2008/09). Employees may also be contracted out of the State scheme, as explained below.

The Additional State Pension is related to your weekly earnings between the weekly Lower and Upper Earnings Limits (£90 and £770 respectively in 2008/09), or credited earnings under the State Second Pension, from April 1978 until the 5th of the April before you reach State Pension age (currently 60 for a woman born on or before 5 April 1950, 65 for a man). These earnings are revalued in line with increases in average earnings.

SERPS

If you reached State Pension age before 6 April 1999, your total revalued earnings were divided by 80 to give the yearly amount of Additional State Pension. This formula provides an Additional State Pension based on 25 per cent of earnings between the specified levels.

However, changes were introduced to phase in, between 1999 and 2009, reductions to the amount of Additional State Pension people receive. The main aim of these changes was to reduce the maximum level of SERPS from 25 per cent of earnings to 20 per cent for people reaching State Pension age from 2009 onwards (with some protection for years up to 1987/88). However, as explained below, the State Second Pension provides a more generous pension to people with low or modest earnings.

FOR MORE INFORMATION, see Pension Service guide NP46 A Guide to State Pensions, which explains how the Additional State Pension is calculated. Copies are only available on the website (www.thepension service.gov.uk).

State Second Pension

Since 6 April 2002 the Additional State Pension has been built up under the State Second Pension. If you have entitlement under SERPS this will be protected, so if you reach(ed) State Pension age on or after 6 April 2003 you may receive an Additional State Pension built up partly under SERPS and partly under the State Second Pension.

Like SERPS, the State Second Pension can provide an Additional State Pension based on your earnings (although in the future it will start to move to becoming a flat-rate pension). However, it is calculated in a way that is more beneficial to those with low and modest earnings.

For this tax year, 2008/09, employees with annual earnings of at least £4,680 but less than £13,500 will be treated as though they have earnings of £13,500.

You will also be treated as though you have earnings of £13,500 if, throughout the year, you are entitled to:

- Carer's Allowance;

- the long-term rate of Incapacity Benefit (or would be if you satisfied the contribution conditions) or Severe Disablement Allowance (for people reaching State Pension age now, credits for those receiving disability benefits are subject to having made a certain number of years of contributions on retirement – although this rule will change in the future); or

23

- Home Responsibilities Protection (HRP – see pages 16–18) because you are looking after a long-term sick or disabled person or a child under the age of six. Usually people will be credited into the State Second Pension automatically, although some people need to claim HRP – when this is the case since 2002/03 you must do this by the end of the third year following the year for which you are claiming HRP.

To qualify for a year of the State Second Pension you must fulfil one of the criteria for a whole tax year – for example, you cannot combine different types of caring responsibilities, or be providing care for part of the year and fulfil the disability conditions for the rest of the year. At current rates you will build up around £1.20 a week of the State Second Pension for each full tax year that you fulfil one of the conditions.

From the tax year 2010/11 onwards, there will be changes that will make it easier for people providing care to build up the State Second Pension. For example, HRP will be replaced by a weekly carer credit available to those caring for a sick or disabled person and people caring for a child up to the age of 12.

Contracting out of the State Second Pension

'Contracting out' means that you leave the Additional State Pension by joining either an occupational pension scheme, a stakeholder pension scheme or another type of personal pension scheme. These schemes have to satisfy certain conditions in order for them to be able to contract out of the State scheme.

If you contract out through your employer's occupational pension scheme, this will provide a pension in place of the Additional State Pension, and both you and your employer will pay a lower rate of NI contributions. If your employer's occupational scheme is not contracted out, both you and your employer will pay full-rate NI contributions and you will build up entitlement to both the full Additional State Pension and the pension due under the rules of your employer's scheme. An adjustment may be made to your occupational pension in respect of any Additional State Pension that you build up during the period that you are a member of your employer's scheme. Contact your employer or the scheme administrator if you need more information.

If you contract out with a personal pension or a stakeholder pension, once a year HM Revenue & Customs will pay a rebate of your NI contributions direct to your pension provider, together with tax relief at the basic rate on your share of the rebate. These payments are known as 'Minimum Contributions'.

FOR MORE INFORMATION, see HM Revenue & Customs leaflet CA17 Employee's Guide to Minimum Contributions. *Copies are only available on the website (www.hmrc.gov.uk).*

Anyone with a personal or stakeholder pension earning below £13,500 in the 2008/09 tax year will receive a 'top-up' of the Additional State Pension irrespective of whether or not they are contracted out. Also, anyone in an occupational pension scheme earning between £4,680 and £31,100 will receive a 'top-up' of the Additional State Pension.

It is a good idea to seek professional financial advice before contracting out, especially if you are considering

25

entering a money-purchase scheme or taking out an appropriate personal pension. It is also important that you continue to review your pension arrangements on a regular basis to ensure that you are making adequate provision for your retirement. Again, you should take advice. Remember, though, that if you choose to see an adviser, you may have to pay for their advice.

For the period April 1978 to April 1997, any estimate of the amount of State Pension that you will receive when you retire will show how much Additional State Pension you have built up during that period. If you were contracted out of SERPS for any time, the statement will show a 'contracted-out deduction' which takes into account the period when you were not paying into SERPS. The amount of Additional State Pension (before the deduction) minus the contracted-out deduction shows how much Additional State Pension will actually be paid on top of your Basic State Pension.

If you are contracted out, you will not build up any Additional State Pension entitlement after 6 April 1997.

Widows, widowers and surviving civil partners

When a widow starts to receive her State Pension at 60, or if she is already receiving her State Pension at the time she is widowed, she can inherit all or some of her late husband's Additional State Pension (adjusted for periods when he was contracted out of SERPS/the State Second Pension). As a widow any amount you are entitled to is added to any Additional State Pension on your own contributions up to the maximum amount of Additional State Pension a single person could receive. Subject to this maximum level, the amount of SERPS pension you can inherit depends on when your husband dies and when he reaches, or was due to reach, State Pension age (65). A woman whose husband died on or before 5 October 2002 inherits all his SERPS pension. She can also inherit all his SERPS pension if he dies after that date but he was born on or before 5 October 1937 (and therefore reached State Pension age on or before 5 October 2002).

If your husband's date of birth is between 6 October 1937 and 5 October 1945, you will be able to inherit between 60 per cent and 90 per cent of his SERPS pension depending on his precise date of birth. If he is due to reach State Pension age on or after 6 October 2010, you will only be able to inherit 50 per cent of his SERPS pension.

Similar rules apply to a widower if both he and his late wife are over State Pension age when she dies. In this case the husband can inherit some or all of his wife's SERPS depending on when she reaches State Pension age (60). He will be able to inherit all his wife's SERPS pension (subject to the maximum level) if she died on or before 5 October 2002, or if she dies after that date but had already reached State Pension age by 5 October 2002. If a man was widowed on or after 9 April 2001, in some circumstances he may be able to inherit his wife's SERPS pension if he is under State Pension age when she dies.

Where a couple are in a civil partnership and one person dies, the surviving partner may be able to inherit his or her partner's SERPS pension in line with the rules set out for widowers.

As explained earlier, for contributions made from April 2002 SERPS has been replaced by the State Second Pension. The maximum amount of the State Second Pension that a widow, widower or surviving civil partner can inherit is 50 per cent, regardless of when they are widowed.

27

A widower or surviving civil partner who was over State Pension age when they were bereaved, but whose late wife or civil partner was under State Pension age when they died, cannot currently inherit Additional State Pension. This will become possible for widowers and surviving civil partners who reach State Pension age after 5 April 2010.

FOR MORE INFORMATION, see Pension Service guide NP46, which includes information about State Pension rights for widows, widowers and surviving civil partners whose spouse/civil partner was contracted out of SERPS/the State Second Pension. Copies are only available on the website (www.thepensionservice.gov.uk). Leaflet SERPSL1 provides information about inheritance of SERPS.

GRADUATED RETIREMENT BENEFIT

This taxable pension scheme, sometimes called 'Graduated Pension', existed from April 1961 to April 1975 and was based on graduated contributions paid from earnings. If you were over 18 during this period and paying graduated contributions, your Graduated Retirement Benefit for the year 2008/09 will be based on these weekly rates:

Women	10.98p for every £9.00 contributions paid
Men	10.98p for every £7.50 contributions paid

This will be paid when you claim your State Pension, normally with the Basic State Pension. However, you can receive Graduated Retirement Benefit even if you do not qualify for a Basic State Pension. Women reaching State Pension age after 5 April 2010 will have their

Graduated Retirement Benefit worked out in the same way as for men.

Married women, widows, widowers and surviving civil partners

In the past, a married woman of 60 or over whose husband had put off drawing his State Pension could have found that claiming a small Graduated Retirement Benefit meant that she did not benefit from an increased married woman's State Pension. However, these rules changed from April 2006. (See pages 33–34 for further information.)

A widow can inherit half her late husband's Graduated Retirement Benefit whether she is over or under State Pension age at the time of bereavement. A widower or surviving civil partner whose wife/civil partner died after 5 April 1979 can also inherit half their late spouse's or civil partner's Graduated Retirement Benefit, provided they were both over State Pension age (currently 60 for women born on or before 5 April 1950, 65 for men) when the late wife/civil partner died. The inheritance rules for widowers and surviving civil partners reaching State Pension age after 5 April 2010 will be the same as for widows.

DEFERRING YOUR STATE PENSION

Once you reach State Pension age you can draw your State Pension if you satisfy the contribution conditions even if you are still working. Alternatively, you can choose to defer (postpone) drawing your State Pension, in which case you can receive extra State Pension or a one-off taxable lump-sum payment at a later date.

If you deferred your State Pension for at least seven weeks before 6 April 2005, then for that period it is increased by about 7.5 per cent for each year of deferment. However, under current rules which were introduced on 6 April 2005, your State Pension will be increased by about 10.4 per cent for each full year you do not draw it or, instead of receiving extra State Pension, you can choose to receive a lump-sum payment along with your normal State Pension. Both the current rules and the old rules are summarised here. If you have a period of deferment both before and after April 2005, then your State Pension will be increased partly according to the old rules and then, for the period of deferment after April 2005, the new rules will apply.

Before April 2005 people could defer their State Pension for a maximum of five years – so they could normally only defer their State Pension up to the age of 65 for women or 70 for men (although there were circumstances when a married woman of 65 or over could defer her State Pension if she had a husband under 70 who was deferring his State Pension). Under the rules from April 2005 onwards, there are no time limits to how long you can defer, so if you wish you can defer your State Pension for more than five years.

You do not have to be working to defer your State Pension but you will not be counted as deferring your State Pension if you are receiving certain other benefits instead. For example, a woman who decides not to draw her State Pension at the age of 60 but to continue to claim Widow's Pension until the age of 65, or someone in receipt of Carer's Allowance, will not gain any extra State Pension. You should also note that if you are entitled to an increase for a dependant (for example because you are a married man with a wife aged under 60) and you defer your State Pension, you will not get any extra State Pension or lump sum for this part of your State Pension.

If you do start drawing your State Pension, it is possible to change your mind and defer it instead. However, this can only be done once, and you must be living in the United Kingdom (there are exemptions to this rule for people living in the European Union and other EEA countries). So, for example, if you are drawing your State Pension (and have not drawn and given it up before), you could choose to stop receiving it and defer it for a period of time in order to benefit from the rules. If you are a married man and your wife is drawing a State Pension based on your contributions, you will need your wife's consent before cancelling your State Pension as she will have to give hers up too.

Increased Basic State Pension for periods before April 2005

If you deferred your State Pension for at least seven weeks before April 2005, when you do choose to draw it, your State Pension will be increased by about 7.5 per cent a year for each full year that you did not draw it. (If you were deferring your State Pension before 6 April 1979, you will have earned a smaller increase.) For each week that you defer your State Pension, it will be increased by one seventh of 1 per cent – this works out as 1 per cent for each seven weeks.

Someone who put off drawing their State Pension for the full five years will have had it increased by about 37.5 per cent.

Deferment for periods after April 2005

Under the current rules, if you defer your State Pension for at least five weeks it will be increased by one fifth of 1 per cent for each week you defer – this works out as 1 per cent for each five weeks. Your State Pension will be increased by around 10.4 per cent for each full year that you do not draw it – so, if you defer your State Pension for five years, it will be increased by just over half. Alternatively, instead of extra State Pension you could receive a taxable lump-sum payment plus your weekly State Pension paid at the normal rate. The lump sum will be calculated based on the amount of State Pension (excluding any State Pension increase for an adult dependant) you have forgone and a compounded interest rate of 2 per cent above the Bank of England base rate. You have to put off claiming your State Pension for at least 12 consecutive months (which cannot include any period before 6 April 2005) to have the choice of a lump-sum payment. As explained above, you will not accrue extra State Pension or a lump-sum payment if you receive certain other benefits or another category of State Pension while you are deferring your State Pension.

If you do not put off drawing your State Pension for a full year, you can receive extra State Pension (as long as you put off drawing it for at least five weeks) or you can receive your State Pension backdated to the time when you could have started to receive it (but without any interest payments).

Increased Additional State Pension and Graduated Retirement Benefit

If you defer drawing your State Pension, your Additional State Pension and Graduated Retirement Benefit will be increased in the same way as the Basic State Pension; or if you opt for a lump-sum payment, they will be included in the calculation of this.

FOR MORE INFORMATION, see Pension Service guides NP46 and SPD2 Deferring your State Pension, or the longer guide SPD1.

Deferment for married women

If you are a married woman entitled to a State Pension on your own contributions and you defer drawing it, the State Pension will be increased (or you can take a one-off lump-sum payment), as described previously.

If you are entitled to a State Pension (or an increase to your State Pension) based on your husband's contributions, currently you can only draw this when your husband claims his own State Pension. If he decides to defer claiming his State Pension, you will not be able to draw any State Pension based on his contributions until he stops deferring his, but when you do draw it you will get extra State Pension (or a lump sum). These rules are due to change in April 2010 – from that date onwards a woman will be able to draw a State Pension based on her husband's record, provided he has reached State Pension age, even if he defers his pension.

In general, you will not get extra State Pension or a lump-sum payment for deferring the State Pension from your husband's contributions if, while your husband is deferring his State Pension, you draw any State Pension you are entitled to on your own contributions or certain other benefits. It may be better not to draw your own State Pension (for example, if this is a small amount) if your husband is deferring his State Pension. However,

33

following a change in the rules on 6 April 2006, if you draw Graduated Retirement Benefit only, it will not stop you getting extra State Pension or a lump-sum payment from your husband's contributions.

Inheritance and divorce

If you die while you are still deferring your State Pension, your surviving spouse or civil partner may be entitled to extra State Pension or a lump-sum payment when they claim their own State Pension. If you are unmarried and not in a civil partnership at the time of your death, the extra State Pension or lump sum cannot be passed on to anyone else.

If you are entitled to a Shared Additional State Pension (resulting from the sharing of a former spouse's or civil partner's Additional State Pension following divorce or dissolution of a civil partnership), you can also defer this.

FOR MORE INFORMATION, see Pension Service guide SPD1 Your Guide to State Pension Deferral or look on the website (at www.thepensionservice. gov.uk/statepensiondeferral/).

Income Tax and the impact on income-related benefits

The State Pension is taxable and is taken into account for benefits such as Pension Credit, Housing Benefit and Council Tax Benefit. If you receive extra State Pension following deferment this will count as part of your taxable income and may reduce the amount of any income-related benefits you receive. However, the lump-sum payment will be ignored if you claim Pension Credit, Housing Benefit or Council Tax Benefit. The lump sum will be taxed at the rate you are currently paying Income Tax on other income (so it will not put you into a higher tax band). You can choose to delay receiving it until the tax year after you start receiving your State Pension, which may be an advantage if your income is lower then.

Deciding what to do

In the past most people chose to draw their State Pension at State Pension age but the more generous rules now may mean that more people will think about deferment. Deferring your claim to State Pension may not be right for everyone, and the amount you could get will depend on your circumstances. If you are interested in putting off claiming your State Pension, it is important to find out more before you decide. Make sure you have full information and get advice if you are not sure about the different options.

For more information, see Pension Service guide SPD1 Your Guide to State Pension Deferral, *which gives information about deferment and the things to consider, and the Age Concern Information Guide* Deferring Retirement Pension, *which is available from the Age Concern Information Line on 0800 00 99 66.*

OVER-80S STATE PENSION

This is a non-contributory taxable State Pension of £54.35 a week for people aged 80 or over who have no State Pension. (It is officially called a 'Category D' pension.) For someone who already gets a State Pension of less than £54.35 a week, an Over-80s State Pension will be paid to bring that State Pension up to this level.

To qualify for this State Pension you have to be living in the UK on the day you became 80 or the date of your claim if this is later, and to have been here for 10 years or more in any 20-year period after your 60th birthday. If you have lived in Gibraltar or another European Union country, this may help you satisfy the conditions.

The Over-80s State Pension will be counted as income in full for the purposes of Pension Credit, Housing Benefit and Council Tax Benefit.

FOR MORE INFORMATION, see DWP claim form (with notes) BR2488.

ENTITLEMENTS BEFORE AND AFTER STATE PENSION AGE

Although State Pension age is currently 60 for women and 65 for men, there is no official retirement age. Some people will stop work before State Pension age and some will work longer, while others may want to retire gradually; for example by reducing their hours rather than leaving work completely. This section summarises the financial support available for people who are not working before State Pension age or who work after that age, referring to other parts of the book where appropriate.

If you are under State Pension age

You cannot draw your State Pension until you reach State Pension age (currently 60 for women born on or before 5 April 1950, 65 for men). However, you may be entitled to other financial support, as summarised here.

If you are working Working Tax Credit can provide additional financial help to people with low incomes who work at least 16 hours a week. (See pages 154–155 for more information.) You may also be entitled to help with your housing costs from Housing and/or Council Tax Benefit.

If you are looking for work If you are able to work and actively seeking a job, you may be entitled to Jobseeker's Allowance, as explained on pages 155–159. You may also be entitled to help with your housing costs from Housing and/or Council Tax Benefit.

If you are unable to work If you are unable to work because of sickness, you may be entitled to Incapacity Benefit, depending on your contribution record (see pages 125–131). If you are a carer, you may be entitled to Carer's Allowance (see pages 120–124). People under the age of 60 who are not required to 'sign on' for work in order to receive benefit may be entitled to Income Support if they have a low income. People over State Pension age and men aged 60–64 can receive Pension Credit without having to be available for work. You may also be entitled to help with your housing costs from Housing and/or Council Tax Benefit.

Occupational and personal pensions You may qualify for some occupational pension before State Pension age (currently 60 for women, 65 for men) if you retire early – check with your employer for details.

You can usually draw a personal pension or stakeholder pension at any time between the ages of 50 and 75. However, if you were contracted out of SERPS/the State Second Pension, you cannot start to receive the part of your personal or stakeholder pension built up from the

37

minimum NI contributions paid into your fund until you reach the age of 60.

The standard minimum age for drawing an occupational or personal pension is due to increase from 50 to 55 by 2010.

Protecting your State Pension If you are under State Pension age and not paying NI contributions, check that you will have enough contributions to receive a full State Pension when you reach State Pension age, by contacting the HM Revenue & Customs National Insurance Contributions Office (see address on page 208).

You will receive credits towards your State Pension if you are drawing a benefit such as Jobseeker's Allowance or Incapacity Benefit. If you are under 60 and seeking work, it may be worth signing on as unemployed – even if you are not entitled to benefit – because you will receive credits. If you are a man aged 60–64, you will normally receive credits automatically even if you are not ill or signing on as unemployed. However, you cannot get these automatic credits for any tax year during which you are abroad for more than six months. If you are not entitled to credits and have an incomplete NI record, you may want to consider paying voluntary contributions.

Working after State Pension age

State Pensions Once you reach State Pension age you can choose to claim your State Pension or to defer it (in other words, postpone drawing it) in order to gain later, as explained on pages 29–35. If you work and draw your State Pension, it will not be affected by the amount you earn or the number of hours you work. You should note, however, that if you are claiming an increase of your

State Pension for a dependent husband or wife, this increase could be affected by their earnings, as explained on pages 7–8.

Although your State Pension will not be reduced because you are working, it is counted as part of your taxable income. Your tax code will be adjusted to take into account the amount of any State Pension (including Additional State Pension and Graduated Retirement Benefit) you receive.

If you carry on working after State Pension age, you will not have to pay NI contributions. You should receive a 'certificate of exception' from HM Revenue & Customs to give to your employer, who will still have to pay contributions for you.

Unemployment and sickness If you have deferred your State Pension, you cannot claim Incapacity Benefit or Jobseeker's Allowance if you become unable to work. This is because neither of these benefits can start to be paid to someone who has reached State Pension age.

Occupational and personal pensions If you have a private pension, you may be able to receive this while you are working – contact your pension scheme for more information.

CHRISTMAS BONUS

The Christmas Bonus of £10 will be paid to people who are entitled to one of the State benefits listed below and who are living in the UK or any other European Union country during the week beginning 1 December 2008. The bonus is tax-free and has no effect on other benefits.

Who qualifies?

You will get the Christmas Bonus if you are receiving:

- a State Pension;

- Over-80s or Widow's Pension;

- Attendance Allowance;

- Disability Living Allowance (any level or component);

- Carer's Allowance;

- Industrial Death Benefit;

- Incapacity Benefit payable at the long-term rate;

- Severe Disablement Allowance;

- Pension Credit;

- War Widow's Pension;

- Unemployability Supplement or Allowance; or

- Constant Attendance Allowance paid with a War or Industrial Disablement Pension.

It is also payable to someone aged 65 or over who receives a War Disablement Pension, but who does not get a qualifying benefit.

Only one bonus can be given to each person. However, someone over State Pension age may get an additional bonus for a dependent spouse or an unmarried partner who is over State Pension age or who reaches State Pension age during the week beginning 1 December 2008 but is not entitled to the bonus in their own right.

How it is paid

There is usually no need to claim, as the bonus is paid automatically. Depending on the way your State Pension is normally paid, the bonus will be added to your State Pension and paid into your account, or sent by cheque. If you think you are entitled to the bonus but do not receive it by the end of December, contact The Pension Service or Jobcentre Plus office that pays your State Pension or benefits.

DECISION-MAKING AND APPEALS

This section outlines the system of decision-making and the way that you can challenge a decision about a State Pension or benefit. There is a different review system for the discretionary Social Fund, which is explained on pages 103–104.

When you receive a letter giving details of whether you have been awarded a benefit, and if so how much, you will also get information about what to do if you disagree with the decision. It is very important to be aware that there are time limits for challenging decisions – take action as soon as possible if you are unhappy with a decision.

If you want to challenge a decision it is often useful to get advice from a local agency, such as Citizens Advice. For example it may be able to advise on whether you have a good case; contact the pension centre on your behalf; prepare your case; and it may perhaps be able to represent you at an appeal tribunal.

Decisions

Most social security decisions are made by the Secretary of State – in practice by a decision-maker in the DWP on behalf of the Secretary of State. Decisions on Housing Benefit and Council Tax Benefit are made by decision-makers in the local authority. In most situations decisions can be revised or superseded or you can take the matter to an appeal tribunal. You should note, however, that the information below does not apply to certain types of decision, such as how benefits are paid. These decisions are not subject to the appeals procedures, although you can still ask for the decision to be reconsidered. For some decisions about contributions you will need to contact HM Revenue & Customs if you disagree with the decision.

Revising and superseding decisions

If you are refused benefit or disagree with the amount awarded, you have one calendar month to ask for the decision to be revised (in other words, to be looked at again and changed). If you have not been given a written 'statement of reasons' for the decision, you can ask for one within the one-month period, in which case the time limit will be extended by 14 days. If the statement arrives outside the one-month period, the 14 days starts from when you receive it. The one-month time limit can also be extended to up to 13 months in certain situations if there are 'special circumstances' for asking for a late revision.

If you are asking for the decision to be revised, send in any additional information that might help. Asking for a revision is intended to be a quick and flexible procedure. You can do this by letter or phone, explaining why you think the decision is wrong – make it clear that you are asking for your benefit to be revised. You will then be sent a letter explaining whether the decision is being revised. If you are still not happy with the decision you can appeal.

Decisions awarding benefit may also be 'superseded' at any time if, for example, your circumstances change or there is new information which affects the decision. Let the DWP know as soon as possible about any information that might affect your benefit. Otherwise you may lose benefit or receive too much and have to repay money.

Appeals

If you have received a decision you disagree with, or you have asked for a decision to be revised and you are not happy with the outcome of that application, you can appeal. You should appeal within one month of the date on the letter about the revision, although this time can be extended to up to 13 months if your appeal has a reasonable prospect of success or there are 'special circumstances' why it is late. If you appeal, the decision will be looked at again to see if it can be revised. If the decision is revised in your favour the appeal will not go ahead, even if you do not get all you asked for. You can appeal against the new decision if you are still unhappy.

Ask for an appeal using the form attached to DWP leaflet GL24 *If You Think Our Decision is Wrong* if possible (although other requests in writing may be accepted), saying which decision you are appealing against and giving the reasons why you disagree with the decision.

Although most appeals will be considered by a tribunal, there is the option for the Tribunals Service to 'strike out' an appeal – for example if you do not provide information requested within the specified time limits. Contact a local agency for help if this happens. When your appeal is accepted you will be sent information and papers relevant to your case. You will be sent a form asking if you wish to attend the tribunal or if you are happy for the appeal to be decided just on the basis of the written information provided. It is important that you return this form within the specified time limit or your appeal may not go ahead. It is always better to attend if possible so as to have an opportunity to explain the position and answer questions.

Tribunals

Appeals are administered by the Tribunals Service, which is an agency of the Department for Constitutional Affairs. Tribunals will consist of one, two or three people, depending on the benefit involved and the issues raised. Tribunal members are independent and one will be a lawyer. There may be an officer from the DWP present.

When you arrive at the tribunal, a clerk will explain the procedures, which are intended to be as informal as possible. You will be given time to put your case and the tribunal will ask questions. The clerk should reimburse your travel expenses before you leave. The tribunal must decide whether the decision was right according to the law, but cannot change a decision just because it seems unfair. You may be told the outcome straightaway; otherwise notification of the decision will be sent to you later.

If you are unhappy with the tribunal's decision, you may be able to make a further appeal to a Social Security Commissioner – seek advice from a local advice agency about how to do this.

FOR MORE INFORMATION, see DWP guide NI260 A Guide to Revision, Supersession and Appeal, which is only available on the website (www.dwp.gov.uk), or the Welfare Benefits and Tax Credits Handbook (see page 211) for more detailed information.

OCCUPATIONAL AND PERSONAL PENSIONS

Occupational pensions are run by employers and are also known as 'company' pensions. Personal pensions and stakeholder pensions are provided by financial institutions, such as banks, building societies and insurance companies.

Employees earning over a certain amount must either pay into the Additional State Pension or be contracted out into an occupational, personal or stakeholder pension, as explained on pages 24–26. Self-employed people do not have access to either the Additional State Pension or to an occupational pension and cannot, therefore, contract out. They can, however, take out a personal pension or a stakeholder pension that is not contracted out of the State scheme.

Stakeholder pensions have been available since April 2001 and are a type of personal pension which must satisfy certain government standards with the aim of providing flexibility and value for money. New pensions called 'Personal Accounts' have been proposed by the Government but these are not due to be introduced until 2012.

It is not within the scope of this book to give information about the different types of pension scheme and, in any case, terms and conditions vary. Contact your scheme provider if you need more information – for example if you need to find out more about provision for widows or other dependants.

FOR MORE INFORMATION if you have paid into one or more pensions in the past and have lost touch with any of the schemes, contact the Pension Tracing Service, The Pension Service, Tyneview Park, Whitley Road, Benton, Newcastle upon Tyne NE98 1BA. Tel: 0845 600 2537. Website: www.thepensionservice.gov.uk

Getting advice

If you have a problem with your pension that you cannot sort out with your employer or pension provider, you can seek advice from the Pensions Advisory Service (TPAS – contact details on page 209) or Citizens Advice. TPAS is an independent voluntary organisation with a network of local advisers who can offer free help and advice. If TPAS cannot resolve your problem, it may recommend that you make a complaint to the Pensions Ombudsman.

FOR MORE INFORMATION, see the DWP leaflets on State Pensions and other pensions. These can be obtained from the Pensions Info Order Line on 0845 731 3233 or the website (www.dwp.gov.uk).

How State benefits are affected

All pensions (State Pensions, occupational pensions, and personal and stakeholder pensions) will be counted as income in full for the purposes of calculating State benefits such as Pension Credit, Income Support, income-based Jobseeker's Allowance (JSA), Housing Benefit and Council Tax Benefit. They can also reduce the amount of contribution-based JSA you get (see page 156) or the amount of Incapacity Benefit paid (see page 129). If you receive a State Pension or benefit and wish to claim an increase for a dependent wife or husband, any occupational, personal or stakeholder pension they receive will be counted as earnings and may affect your increase, as explained on pages 7–8.

Income-Related (Means-Tested) Benefits

This part of *Your Rights* describes the benefits that people aged 60 or over may be able to claim based on their income and savings. It covers Pension Credit, Housing Benefit and Council Tax Benefit, which are weekly entitlements, and the Discretionary Social Fund, which provides lump-sum payments for exceptional expenses.

Many older people are not claiming their entitlements. Pension Credit was introduced in October 2003. Although it has been widely advertised, and the Government has been encouraging older people to claim, many are still missing out. There are also up to 2 million pensioners who are not claiming the Council Tax Benefit that is due to them. Homeowners are particularly likely to be missing out; perhaps because they incorrectly believe that they are not entitled to help because they own their own homes. So if you are aged 60 or over, make sure that you are not missing out on the income that is due to you.

PENSION CREDIT

Pension Credit is a weekly social security entitlement for people aged 60 and over with low and modest incomes. You do not need to have paid National Insurance (NI) contributions to qualify for Pension Credit, but your income and any savings and capital over a certain level will be taken into account. Pension Credit does not have an upper capital limit. It is not taxable.

It has two parts – the guarantee credit and the savings credit. The guarantee credit helps with weekly basic living expenses by topping up your income to a level set by the Government. The savings credit provides additional cash to people aged 65 and over who have income over a certain level, from sources such as pensions and savings. People may be entitled to the guarantee credit or the savings credit or both.

If you receive Pension Credit and you are liable to pay rent and/or Council Tax, then you are also likely to qualify for Housing Benefit and/or Council Tax Benefit to help with these bills. Even if your income is too high for you to receive Pension Credit, then you may still be entitled to Housing Benefit and Council Tax Benefit. (See pages 76–99 for more information.)

Pension Credit can be paid to homeowners, tenants, and people in other circumstances such as living with family or friends. You can work and receive Pension Credit, although most of your earnings will be taken into account. Once you get Pension Credit, you may also be able to apply for other benefits such as lump-sum payments from the Social Fund (see pages 99–104), while if you are entitled to the guarantee credit this will 'passport' you to help with health costs such as help towards glasses (see pages 182–184) and free dental treatment (see pages 181–182).

People under State Pension age who are seeking work may be entitled to Jobseeker's Allowance (see pages 155–159), while those under 60 who are not able to work, for example due to caring responsibilities or incapacity, may be entitled to Income Support (see pages 159–160). This book does not provide detailed information about the income-related benefits available to people under the age of 60, so if you need further information contact a local advice agency or Jobcentre Plus office.

Who qualifies?

You may receive Pension Credit if you fulfil all the following conditions:

- you are aged 60 or over (65 for the savings credit);

- your income is below a certain level; and

- you are habitually resident in the UK and you are not excluded from claiming benefit because of your immigration status. Contact a local advice agency if you need further advice about the benefit position for people who have been living abroad.

Couples For a couple, one of you applies on behalf of both partners – the person who applies must be aged at least 60, although their partner can be younger. For savings credit at least one of a couple must have reached 65. A 'partner' is the person you are married to or living with as if you are married, or your civil partner or the person you are living with as if you are civil partners. If you live with someone who is not your partner – such as a friend or a brother or sister – you are assessed separately and both of you can apply for Pension Credit.

How to work it out

To work out if you are entitled to Pension Credit you will need to use the following steps, which are explained below:

1 Add up the value of your savings and, if you have more than £6,000, work out the 'assumed income'.

2 Add up your weekly income, ignoring any types of income which are not taken into account.

3 Check the 'appropriate amount' for someone in your circumstances – this is the minimum level of income you are expected to live on.

4 Work out the difference between your income and the appropriate amount to see if you are entitled to guarantee credit.

5 If you (or your partner if you have one) are aged 65 or over, check if you are entitled to savings credit by working out your 'qualifying income' and following the calculation set out below.

1 Your savings

Throughout this book the term 'savings' is used to cover savings, capital, investments and property. Savings are assessed in the same way for both the guarantee credit and the savings credit. Some forms of savings, including your home if you own it, are not taken into account, as explained below.

For Pension Credit, up to £6,000 savings, and any income you receive from these savings, is ignored (the amount ignored is £10,000 for people in care homes).

For a couple, savings are added together, but the limit is the same. There is no upper savings limit for Pension Credit but any savings over £6,000 will be counted as £1 a week 'assumed income' for every £500 (or part of £500) over £6,000. For example, if you have £7,200 this will be counted as a weekly income of £3 a week, while savings of £13,600 will be assessed as an income of £16 a week.

Savings are normally valued at their current market or surrender value. If there are expenses involved in selling them, 10 per cent will be deducted. Most forms of savings and capital will be taken into account, including:

- cash;
- bank and building society accounts (including current accounts that do not pay interest);
- National Savings accounts and certificates (valued according to rules which The Pension Service will explain);
- premium bonds;
- income bonds;
- stocks and shares;
- property (other than your home); and
- a share of any savings you own jointly with other people – these will normally be divided equally by the number of joint owners to calculate your share (get advice if you need to value your share of a jointly-owned property).

Some types of savings will be ignored, including:

- the value of your home if you own it and are living there;

- the surrender value of a life assurance policy (although if a policy is cashed in the money you receive will normally be counted);

- arrears of certain benefits, such as Attendance Allowance, Disability Living Allowance or Income Support, are normally ignored for 52 weeks from the date you receive them (or if the arrears are £5,000 or over and due to an official error, they may be able to be ignored for as long as you are getting Pension Credit);

- a lump-sum payment received because you deferred drawing your State Pension for 52 weeks or more;

- your personal possessions; and

- the £10,000 ex-gratia payment for Far Eastern Prisoners of War (see page 135).

There are also other forms of savings not listed here which are ignored and there are circumstances when property or savings will not be taken into account for a certain period of time.

FOR MORE INFORMATION, see the DWP guide to Pension Credit, which is only available on the website (www.thepensionservice.gov.uk).

Deprivation of capital (notional capital) If you 'deprive' yourself of savings in order to get benefit or to increase the amount of benefit, you will be treated as still having those savings. This is known as 'notional capital'.

This might occur if you give money to your family or buy expensive items in order to gain benefit. However, you will not be assessed as having notional capital if you have paid off debts or if your spending was 'reasonable' in your circumstances. You should seek advice if you are refused benefit because of notional capital.

2 Your income

This section explains how your income is assessed for the guarantee credit. For the savings credit you will also need this figure but, as explained later, if you have certain types of income they will be deducted from the total. The main types of income that are counted and the main types of income, or parts of income, that are ignored are listed below. If you have any income from other sources, you will need to check whether or not they are included. Income is assessed after tax and NI contributions have been paid. (If you receive income without tax deducted but are due to pay tax on this at a later date, get advice.) For a couple, the income of both partners is added together.

Income that is taken into account includes:

- State Pensions;
- occupational and personal pensions;
- income from annuities;
- most social security benefits (but see below for some exceptions);
- earnings (but see below for amounts ignored);
- Working Tax Credit;
- income from boarders or sub-tenants (but see below for parts ignored);

55

- regular payments from equity release schemes;

- maintenance payments from a spouse or former spouse; and

- assumed income from savings over £6,000.

Income that will be fully ignored includes:

- Housing Benefit and Council Tax Benefit;

- Attendance Allowance;

- Disability Living Allowance;

- Social Fund payments;

- actual interest or income from savings or capital (interest is not counted as income but once it is paid into an account it will be counted as part of your savings);

- the special War Widow's Pension for 'pre-1973 widows', which is now £73.64 (in addition to the £10 of a War Widow's Pension outlined below); and

- voluntary or charitable payments – for example money given to you by a charity, family or friends.

The following are examples of parts of weekly income that will also be ignored:

- £5 of your earnings if you work and are single;

- £10 of your or your partner's earnings from work (if you both work the maximum is still £10);

- £20 of earnings if you work and you are a carer receiving the carer addition or in certain circumstances when you or your partner is disabled (instead of the £5 or £10 listed above);

- £10 of a War Widow/Widower's Pension or War Disablement Pension; and

- £20 of any payment from a sub-tenant or boarder, and, in the case of a boarder, half of any payment over £20.

Add up your total weekly income, including assumed income from savings over £6,000 but not including any types, or parts, of income that are ignored, to give the weekly income used to work out your guarantee credit.

Qualifying income for savings credit For savings credit, only 'qualifying income' is counted. This is the same as the income used to assess guarantee credit but with the following types of income deducted:

- Incapacity Benefit;

- Severe Disablement Allowance;

- contribution-based Jobseeker's Allowance;

- Working Tax Credit; and

- maintenance payments from a spouse or former spouse.

Most older people tend not to have these sources of income, so all their assessed income is likely to be qualifying income. When this is the case, the same figure is used to work out both the guarantee and savings credit. However, if you do have one or more of the types of non-qualifying income outlined above (such as Incapacity Benefit), remember that this affects the way that your savings credit is worked out.

3 The 'appropriate amount'

This is the minimum amount of income that someone is considered to need for their day-to-day living expenses. It is officially called the 'appropriate minimum guarantee' but is often described as the 'appropriate amount', which is the term used in this book.

If your income is below the appropriate amount for someone in your circumstances, then you will receive the guarantee credit to bring your income up to this level. For many people a 'standard amount' will apply (officially called the 'standard minimum guarantee') but the appropriate amount can include additional amounts for severe disability, for carers and for certain housing costs. It is possible to receive both the carer and the severe disability addition – for example a disabled couple who provide a substantial amount of care for each other could receive both.

The standard appropriate amounts are:

Single person	£124.05
Couple	£189.35

Additional amount for severe disability/severe disability premium Within Pension Credit an addition can be added to your standard minimum amount if you fulfil the conditions described below. For Housing and Council Tax Benefit it is called the 'severe disability premium' but the rates and rules are the same. The rates are:

Single person	£50.35
Couple, one person qualifying	£50.35
Couple, both qualifying	£100.70

As a single person you qualify if:

- you receive Attendance Allowance or the middle or highest level of the care component of Disability Living Allowance (DLA);

- you 'live alone' (but see below for the exceptions to this); and

- no one receives Carer's Allowance (which used to be called Invalid Care Allowance) for looking after you.

If you have a partner and you receive Attendance Allowance (or the middle or highest level of the care component of DLA), you will not normally be able to receive this addition because you will not be counted as 'living alone'. However, you can receive it if:

- your partner also gets Attendance Allowance (or the middle or highest level of the care component of DLA) or he or she is registered blind; and

- no one receives Carer's Allowance for looking after you; and

- you 'live alone'; in other words, there is no-one else living with you and your partner other than a person who is not taken into account, as described below.

If your partner also receives Attendance Allowance (or the middle or highest level of the care component of DLA) and neither of you has a carer receiving Carer's Allowance, you will receive the double rate.

Living alone You will still be counted as living alone in some circumstances when you live with other people. For example, you can still get this addition if there is someone

59

else in your household who also gets Attendance Allowance (or the middle or highest level of the care component of DLA), or someone who is registered blind, or a paid helper supplied by a charity, or in some cases where you are a joint tenant or joint owner and share the housing costs. If you are not sure if you qualify, seek further advice as the rules can be complicated.

Additional amount for carers/carer premium Within Pension Credit a carer addition can be added to your standard amount if you fulfil the conditions described below. For Housing and Council Tax Benefit it is called the 'carer premium' but the rates and rules are the same.

The rates are:

Single person	£27.75
Couple, one person qualifying	£27.75
Couple, both qualifying	£55.50

This addition is available to carers who are receiving Carer's Allowance (see pages 120–124). It will also be given to people who have applied for the allowance and fulfil all the conditions but cannot receive it because they are getting another benefit instead. There is no upper age limit for applying for Carer's Allowance.

For example, if you are receiving a State Pension of £90.70 a week, you cannot be paid Carer's Allowance as well. However, if you apply for Carer's Allowance, you may receive a letter saying that you are entitled to Carer's Allowance but cannot be paid it, which you can show to The Pension Service (for Pension Credit) or the council (for Housing and Council Tax Benefit), so that they can award you the addition/premium.

The carer addition/premium continues to be paid for eight weeks after the person you care for dies, or you cease being a carer for some other reason.

Effect on the disabled person's benefits If the person you care for receives the severe disability addition/premium (see above), and you are paid Carer's Allowance, they will lose the addition/premium when you receive your first payment of Carer's Allowance. You might be able to receive an extra £27.75 a week through the carer addition/premium while the person you care for could lose an addition/premium worth £50.35. However, they will not lose the addition/premium if you are entitled to Carer's Allowance but cannot be paid it because you are receiving a State Pension or another benefit. If you are not sure whether to claim Carer's Allowance or not, get advice first.

4 Calculating your guarantee credit

Once you have worked out your appropriate amount – in other words, the standard amount of £124.05 a week for a single person or £189.35 a week for a couple, plus any additional amounts because you are a carer, severely disabled or have eligible housing costs (see page 64) – compare this figure with your income.

If your income (including assumed income from savings) is less than your appropriate amount, you will receive guarantee credit to bring your income up to this level. If your qualifying income is more than the 'savings credit threshold' – £91.20 a week for a single person, £145.80 for a couple – and you (or your partner) are aged 65 or over, you will also receive savings credit.

If your income is more than your appropriate amount, you will not get guarantee credit but you may still be entitled to Housing Benefit and/or Council Tax Benefit and, if you or your partner are aged 65 or over, to savings credit.

Example

Rose Williams is aged 76, and lives alone in a council flat. Her income is the State Pension of £90.70 a week and an occupational pension of £10. She has savings of £950.

Rose adds up her income

State Pension	£90.70
Occupational pension	£10.00
Total	£100.70

Her appropriate amount is the standard amount for a single person (£124.05).

Rose's income of £100.70 a week is less than her appropriate amount of £124.05. The difference is £23.35. This is how much guarantee credit she will get on top of her State Pension.

Rose is also entitled to some savings credit (see page 67) and to Housing Benefit and Council Tax Benefit to cover all her rent and Council Tax.

Example

Bill and Mary McConnell are a married couple both aged 70. Their joint State Pensions come to £145.05 and Bill gets a pension of £50.10 a week from his old job. They live in their own home and they have savings of £13,000.

Bill and Mary add up their income

State Pension	£145.05
Occupational pension	£50.10
Weekly assumed income from savings	£14.00
Total	£209.15

Their appropriate amount is the standard amount for a couple (£189.35).

Their income of £209.15 is more than their appropriate amount of £189.35, so they do not qualify for guarantee credit. However, they will be entitled to savings credit (see page 67) and Council Tax Benefit to get help with their Council Tax payments.

Example

Andrew Jennings is 80 and lives alone in his own home. His State Pension (Basic and Additional) is £100.95 and he has an occupational pension of £69.20 a week. His savings are less than £6,000. In May 2007 he applied for Pension Credit but was turned down because his income was too high, although he received some Council Tax Benefit. In October 2007 he had a stroke. He now has difficulty with getting dressed and washed but has been able to continue to live on his own with support. No one receives Carer's Allowance for looking after him. His local Age Concern helped him claim Attendance Allowance and reapply for Pension Credit.

Andrew's income, ignoring the Attendance Allowance

State Pension	£100.95
Occupational pension	£69.20
Total	£170.15

63

Andrew's appropriate amount

Standard amount	£124.05
Severe disability addition	£50.35
Total	£174.40

His income is £4.25 less than his appropriate amount, so he receives £4.25 guarantee credit. He can now also receive the maximum amount of savings credit (£19.71) and Council Tax Benefit to cover all his Council Tax.

Help with housing costs

In addition to your standard amount and any additions if you are a carer or severely disabled, your Pension Credit appropriate amount can also include an additional sum for certain housing costs for those who own their property. For tenants, rent and service charges can be covered by Housing Benefit. These additions for homeowners are not included in the applicable amount for Council Tax Benefit. Subject to the restrictions below, if you are aged 60 or over the housing costs which can be included are:

- mortgage interest;
- interest on a loan for certain repairs or improvements;
- ground rent; and
- certain service charges (but funding for support services comes through the 'Supporting People' scheme – see pages 142–143).

If the loan is for more than £100,000 or your housing costs are considered too high (taking into account your situation), the amount added to the appropriate amount may be restricted. Payment is only made towards the eligible mortgage interest and does not cover any payments towards arrears, capital or endowment policies. Claimants may have to meet any shortfall in payments, when their lender's interest rate is higher than the Standard Rate, which is used to calculate eligible mortgage interest payments. Payment towards the eligible mortgage interest is generally made direct to a claimant's lender, provided they are participating in the Mortgage Interest Direct Scheme.

If you are receiving Pension Credit (or other income-related benefits such as Income Support or income-based Jobseeker's Allowance) or have been receiving any of these within the previous 26 weeks, you may only receive help towards any new housing costs in very limited circumstances. You should seek advice before taking out a loan.

Deductions for people living in your home The help provided towards your housing costs may be reduced if there is someone else living in your home apart from your partner or a dependent child. This is because people such as adult sons and daughters (often called 'non-dependants') are expected to contribute to housing costs. Deductions are made according to the age, circumstances and gross income of the non-dependant. However, no reduction will be made in certain circumstances – for example, if you or your partner is blind or you or your partner receives Attendance Allowance or the care component of Disability Living Allowance.

If you are 65 or over, changes due to non-dependants that would reduce your benefit should not apply until 26 weeks after the change of circumstances.

In certain circumstances a deduction will not apply. For example, there are no deductions if the person living with you: is a boarder or a full-time student; is receiving Pension Credit; or is under 25 and receiving Income Support or income-based Jobseeker's Allowance.

The level of the deduction will depend on the age, circumstances and gross weekly income of the non-dependant. For example, if the person living with you is aged 18 or over, works 16 hours a week or more, does not receive Pension Credit and has an income of at least £116 a week, the following deductions will be made:

Gross income of non-dependant	*Weekly deduction*
£116.00 to £171.99	£17.00
£172.00 to £222.99	£23.35
£223.00 to £295.99	£38.20
£296.00 to £368.99	£43.50
£369.00 or more	£47.75

For others aged 18 or over, the deduction will be £7.40. If there is a couple living with you, only one deduction will be made.

Example

Marie Wilson is aged 64 and has a mortgage. Her mortgage interest is assessed as £30 a week, so her appropriate amount is worked out in the following way:

Standard amount	£124.05
Weekly mortgage interest	£30.00
Total	£154.05

Her daughter, who is 35, and earns £190 a week, comes to live with her. There will therefore be a deduction of £23.35 from the amount allowed for mortgage interest. Marie's total Pension Credit appropriate amount will then be reduced to £130.70. This means that she will receive guarantee credit if her total assessed income is less than this amount. She is under 65 and so is not entitled to savings credit.

5 Calculating your savings credit

If you (or your partner if you have one) are aged 65 or over, you may be entitled to savings credit, either in addition to guarantee credit or on its own. The maximum amount of savings credit you can receive is £19.71 for a single person or £26.13 for a couple. This section outlines how the savings credit is worked out and gives some examples. However, the calculation is quite complicated and the examples do not cover all circumstances. If you are not sure whether you qualify, you may want to apply anyway. Alternatively, The Pension Service or a local advice agency may be able to give you an idea of any possible entitlement, or, if you have access to the internet, you could look at the Pension Credit calculator on The Pension Service website (www.thepensionservice.gov.uk).

As a guide, if you are single and your appropriate amount is the standard amount of £124.05, you are likely to be entitled to savings credit if your weekly qualifying income is more than £91.20 and less than around £174. For a couple with a standard amount of £189.35, you will be likely to qualify if your weekly qualifying income is more than £145.80 and less than around £255. The closer your income is to these upper amounts the less savings credit you will receive.

If your appropriate amount is more than the standard amounts (because you get an addition for severe disability, caring or housing costs), you may get savings credit if your income is higher than £174 (single person) or £255 (couple).

To calculate your savings credit you need to know the following things:

1 Your 'income'. This is the income used to calculate guarantee credit – in other words, your total income including assumed income from savings but not including types of income which are ignored, such as Attendance Allowance.

2 Your 'qualifying income'. This is your income as explained above minus any Incapacity Benefit, Severe Disablement Allowance, contribution-based Jobseeker's Allowance, Working Tax Credit and maintenance payments from a spouse or former spouse.

3 Your appropriate amount, as explained above.

4 The 'savings credit threshold', which is £91.20 for a single person and £145.80 for a couple (the threshold used to be the same levels as the Basic State Pension but from April 2008 these figures are no longer the same).

5 The maximum amount of savings credit you can receive, which is £19.71 for a single person or £26.13 for a couple.

Standard appropriate amount The information in this section explains how to calculate your savings credit if your appropriate amount is the standard amount of £124.05 (single person) or £189.35 (couple). If your qualifying income is below £91.20 (single person) or £145.80 (couple), you will not be entitled to savings credit – otherwise one of paragraphs a), b) or c) will apply to you.

a) **If your income is less than your appropriate amount and your qualifying income is above £91.20 (single person) or £145.80 (couple), you will be entitled to savings credit.** Your savings credit will be 60 per cent of the difference between your qualifying income and £91.20 if you are single or £145.80 if you have a partner, up to the maximum amounts. (Another way of saying this is that you will receive 60p for every £1 of qualifying income you have over the threshold.)

Example

On page 62, **Rose Williams** has a Basic State Pension of £90.70 and an occupational pension of £10 a week. Her savings credit will be worked out like this:

Qualifying income	£100.70
Difference between income of £100.70 and savings threshold of £91.20	£9.50
Savings credit is 60% of £9.50 (the difference)	£5.70

Rose will receive £5.70 savings credit in addition to her £23.35 guarantee credit and her pensions of £100.70, making her total income £129.75.

b) **If your qualifying income is exactly £124.05 (single person) or £189.35 (couple), you will normally receive the maximum savings credit**, which is £19.71 for a single person and £26.13 for a couple. (If you also have some non-qualifying income, you will receive less.)

c) If all your income is qualifying income and it is more than £124.05 (single person) or £189.35 (couple), you will receive savings credit if your income is less than a certain amount, which is around £174 for a single person and £255 for a couple. The closer your income is to these levels the less savings credit you will receive. The maximum savings credit of £19.71 for a single person, and £26.13 for a couple, will be reduced by 40 per cent of the difference between your income and £124.05 (single person) or £189.35 (couple). (Another way of saying this is that the maximum savings credit is reduced by 40 pence for every pound of income you have above these levels.)

Example

In the example on page 62, **Bill and Mary McConnell** cannot get guarantee credit because their income of £209.15 is more than £189.35 (their appropriate amount). Their savings credit is worked out like this:

Qualifying income	£209.15
Difference between their income and £189.35	£19.80
40% of this difference	£7.92
Their savings credit is the maximum savings credit of £26.13 minus £7.92 (40% of the difference)	£18.21

Appropriate amount above the standard amount If you receive an addition for severe disability, caring or housing costs (like Andrew Jennings in the example on page 63), you can receive savings credit at higher levels

of income. (Examples are not given here but are
included in the Age Concern Factsheet on Pension
Credit.) It is worked out like this:

- If all your income is qualifying income and it is
  more than £91.20 (single person) or £145.80
  (couple) but less than your appropriate amount,
  your savings credit will be 60% of the difference
  between your income and £91.20 (single person)
  or £145.80 (couple) up to the maximum amount of
  savings credit of £19.71 (single person) or £26.13
  (couple).

- If all your income is qualifying income and it is
  the same as or more than the standard amount
  (£124.05 single person, £189.35 couple) but less
  than your appropriate amount, you will receive the
  maximum savings credit.

- If all your income is qualifying income and it is
  more than your appropriate amount, the maximum
  savings credit of £19.71 (single person) or £26.13
  (couple) is reduced by 40% of the difference
  between your income and your appropriate
  amount. If the 40% is more than the maximum,
  you will not receive savings credit.

If you have non-qualifying income If you or your
partner receive non-qualifying income, such as
Incapacity Benefit or Severe Disablement Allowance,
you may still receive savings credit as long as you have
qualifying income over the savings credit threshold
(£91.20 single person, £145.80 couple). However, the
calculation is done a little differently. Contact The
Pension Service or an advice agency if you need more
information about this or look at the example in the

Pension Service technical guide for Pension Credit, which is available on the website (www.thepensionservice.gov.uk).

Pension Credit for people in different circumstances

Living in someone else's home If you live in someone else's home as a member of their household – for example, with your son or daughter – Pension Credit will be worked out in the normal way.

Boarders and hostel dwellers If you are living in a hotel, guest house or hostel, or in board and lodgings, Pension Credit will be worked out in the normal way. You can claim Housing Benefit towards the rental element of your charges and some services. You will have to pay for meals, fuel and other items that are not covered by Housing Benefit from your weekly Pension Credit.

If you go into hospital Since April 2005, if you go into hospital your State Pension can continue to be paid however long you are there and the Pension Credit standard minimum amount is not affected. However, if you receive a severe disability addition or carer addition, you may lose it as these additions are linked to benefits, such as Attendance Allowance and Carer's Allowance, which can be affected by a hospital stay. This will reduce your Pension Credit or in some cases it may stop because without the addition you may no longer qualify for the benefit.

If you go abroad If you go abroad for a temporary stay, Pension Credit will normally stop after four weeks. However, the Government has announced that it will extend this period to 13 weeks. It is expected that this will come into effect in October 2008. If you are planning to go abroad, contact The Pension Service to find out more about your position.

Care homes Pension Credit for people in care homes is generally calculated as described here but see pages 147–150 for the differences.

How to claim Pension Credit

You can claim Pension Credit in a number of ways. There is a special Pension Credit application line on Freephone 0800 99 1234. Staff will help you apply over the phone and will let you know what happens next, or if you prefer you can ask to be sent a form to be filled in. If English is not your first language, you (or someone on your behalf) can ring and arrangements will be made for an interpreter. You can also write for a claim form or obtain it from the internet (at www.thepensionservice.gov.uk). If you would like to have face-to-face help with the form, contact a local advice agency or the local Pension Service.

You may need to provide information to support your claim, such as details of your savings and private pensions. The Pension Service is encouraging people to take up their entitlement to Pension Credit, so it may contact you to ask if you would like more information or to make an application.

Backdating At the time of writing Pension Credit can be backdated for up to 12 months, as long as you have fulfilled the conditions throughout that time. The Government has stated, however, that it will reduce this period – from October 2008 claims will only be backdated for up to three months.

Changes of circumstances and reassessments

When you are awarded Pension Credit you may be told that an 'assessed income period' has been set. This will mean that for the time stated (normally a period of up to five years) you will not need to report changes in your 'retirement provision'. By retirement provision The Pension Service means income from sources such as pensions, annuities, regular payments from an equity release scheme, and savings. Adjustments will be made automatically for regular increases, such as an annual increase in your State or private pension if this happens. If you have a private pension you will be asked if and how it is increased when you apply.

You will not need to tell The Pension Service about changes such as an increase in your savings. However, if your income from these sources goes down, you can contact The Pension Service which will reassess your benefit and may increase the amount of Pension Credit. You still need to report other changes in circumstances, such as getting married, moving house, a change in earnings, or starting to receive certain social security benefits.

An assessed income period will not be set if you (or your partner) are not aged 65 or over. Even if you are over 65 you may not have an assessed income period in some circumstances; for example if your situation is expected to change in the next year. Sometimes a period of less than five years is set. At the end of an assessed income period your Pension Credit will be reassessed.

The Government plans to change the rules so that in the future people aged 75 and over applying for Pension Credit will generally be given an assessed income period which lasts indefinitely and those whose assessed income period runs out after the age of 80 will not normally need to be reassessed. This change is subject to the legislation being agreed but is expected to come into force in April 2009. As with the current system, there are some changes in circumstances that will still bring an assessed income period to an end.

If you are not given an assessed income period, you will need to report any changes in circumstances that may affect your benefit. When Pension Credit is awarded you will be given information about what changes in circumstances you need to report.

How it is paid

Pension Credit is paid weekly and is normally paid with the State Pension – see pages 19–20 for information about the way that pensions and benefits are paid.

If you disagree with a decision

If you disagree with a decision that has been made about your Pension Credit, you can ask for the decision to be revised or appeal against the decision (see pages 41–45). You also have the right to ask for more detailed information about why a decision was made.

FOR MORE INFORMATION, see the Age Concern Factsheet on Pension Credit, which is available from the Age Concern Information Line on 0800 00 99 66, and Pension Service leaflet PC1L Pension Credit *or the more detailed guide PC10S.*

HOUSING BENEFIT AND COUNCIL TAX BENEFIT

Housing Benefit is a social security benefit which provides help with rent, with certain service charges and, in Northern Ireland, with general rates. People who live in Northern Ireland and require information about rate rebates or the new Rate Relief Scheme should contact Age Concern Northern Ireland at the address on page 222.

Council Tax Benefit is a social security benefit which provides help in reducing your Council Tax. See also 'Help with the Council Tax' on pages 176–178, which gives information about other ways your Council Tax bill may be reduced which are not related to your income or savings. The information here only applies to people aged 60 and over. The rules are different for younger people, so if you are under 60 contact your council or a local advice agency for more information.

Housing Benefit and Council Tax Benefit are based on your income and savings. In general, you must have no more than £16,000 in savings, although the limit does not apply to people receiving the guarantee part of the Pension Credit or the second adult rebate within the Council Tax Benefit system. You must also be 'habitually resident' in the UK, and not excluded from claiming because of your immigration status. Housing Benefit and Council Tax Benefit are not taxable.

If you have a partner, the amount of benefit you get will be worked out on your combined savings and income. A 'partner' is the person you are married to or living with as if you are married, or your civil partner or the person you are living with as if you are civil partners. If you live with someone who is not your partner – such as a friend or a brother or sister – you are assessed separately and both of you can apply for help with your housing costs or Council Tax.

Who qualifies for Housing Benefit?

You may get Housing Benefit if you are responsible for paying rent and you fulfil the conditions outlined above.

Benefit is available to council, housing association and private tenants and to people in the following circumstances:

- **Boarders and people living in hostels** may get Housing Benefit for the accommodation part of their charges.

- **People living in a houseboat** may get benefit for the mooring charges even if they own the houseboat.

- **People living in a caravan or mobile home** may get help with the site charges even if they own the caravan or mobile home.

- **Joint tenants** may receive Housing Benefit towards the part of the costs for which they are responsible.

- **People living with a landlord who is a close relative** may claim Housing Benefit if they live separately in self-contained accommodation. However, they cannot claim benefit if they are part of the same household, or if it is not a 'commercial arrangement'. Get advice if you are unsure about your position.

Who qualifies for Council Tax Benefit?

There are two types of Council Tax Benefit – 'main Council Tax Benefit' and 'second adult rebate'. If you are responsible for paying the Council Tax, you may be able to receive main Council Tax Benefit provided that you fulfil the conditions outlined above. If you are jointly responsible for a bill with someone other than your partner, you can apply for help with your share of the tax.

The second adult rebate may be available to some people, regardless of their income and savings, who have one or more people with low incomes living with them. This is covered on pages 94–95, while the rest of this section covers the main benefit scheme.

How to work out your benefit

Housing Benefit and Council Tax Benefit are worked out using similar calculations. The rules outlined below apply to both benefits unless stated otherwise. The rules for working out Housing Benefit, Council Tax Benefit and Pension Credit are broadly similar but there are some differences.

To work out how much benefit you will get, follow the steps listed, which are then explained:

1 Calculate the maximum weekly rent and Council Tax for which you can get benefit.

2 Deduct an amount for any non-dependants living in your home.

3 Add up the value of your savings, but note that certain types of savings are ignored.

4 Add up your weekly income, but note that certain kinds of income are ignored.

5 Work out the amount the Government says you need to live on, called the 'applicable amount'.

6 Calculate your benefit according to the formula explained below.

7 For Housing Benefit, check that the benefit is above the minimum amount payable, which is 50p a week. There is no minimum payment for Council Tax Benefit.

If you are receiving Pension Credit guarantee credit, you don't need to work out your savings, income and applicable amount, as you will receive the maximum eligible benefit minus any deductions for non-dependants.

1 Your rent and Council Tax

For Housing Benefit purposes, rent is the payment made to occupy your home. It also covers certain service charges – for example for furniture, cleaning communal areas, entry phones and rubbish removal. Since April 2003 other support services, such as wardens and community alarms, are funded separately through a system called 'Supporting People'. Local authorities receive a grant for funding support services, including those provided by wardens in retirement (sheltered) housing. (See pages 142–143 for how you get help with your support services.)

Local Housing Allowance is a new way of calculating rent for Housing Benefit purposes. It has already been piloted in some areas and is due to be introduced nationally on 7 April 2008 for all new claims for Housing Benefit for tenants renting accommodation from a private landlord. It also affects tenants already getting Housing Benefit who move into accommodation rented from a private landlord. If you live in council accommodation or social housing, Local Housing

Allowance will not affect you. With Local Housing Allowance, the rent on which your benefit is based will depend on who you live with and the area where you live, rather than the actual rent your landlord charges.

You cannot get benefit for water rates and sewerage charges. Homeowners cannot get Housing Benefit; however, they may get help with mortgage interest payments and certain other housing costs from Pension Credit or income-based Jobseeker's Allowance (see pages 64–66).

If you are a council or housing association tenant, the maximum Housing Benefit you can get is 100 per cent of your assessed rent, including the service charges described above. However, the level of rent on which benefit is calculated may be reduced, as explained below.

High rents If you have been receiving Housing Benefit as a private tenant and you are not covered by the Local Housing Allowance rules, then your benefit may have been restricted. This might have happened if the local authority considered that your rent was too high or your accommodation is larger than you need (taking into account your circumstances) or that the rent has increased unreasonably while you have been getting Housing Benefit.

The system is different for private tenants who are now covered by the Local Housing Allowance, although restrictions may still apply to housing association tenants if the local authority decides that your accommodation is larger than you need or the rent is unreasonably high. Before taking up a tenancy, you can ask the local authority for a 'pretenancy determination', which will tell you how much of the rent would be eligible for

Housing Benefit. Local authorities can make 'discretionary housing payments' if you need help with your rent or Council Tax. So if your benefit is restricted, you may want to apply for help under this scheme.

If you want to challenge a decision about your benefit or to ask the local authority to use its discretion, it is a good idea to get advice from a local agency. The rules on rent restrictions are complicated and are only covered briefly here. If you need more information, contact Age Concern or consult a book such as the *Welfare Benefits and Tax Credits Handbook* (see page 211).

Council Tax The maximum Council Tax Benefit you can get is 100 per cent of your bill.

Council Tax Benefit is based on the amount you are asked to pay after any 'discounts' or 'reductions' (see pages 176–178) have been given. For example, if you live alone you will receive a 25 per cent discount on your bill, and your benefit will be worked out after this has been deducted.

Note that the calculations in this section are all done on a weekly basis. So if you pay your Council Tax in ten monthly instalments, you will first have to work out how much this would be per week over the whole year.

Heating charges Some people have a charge for heating included in their rent. You cannot get Housing Benefit for heating and other fuel charges. If, for example, you pay £45 a week rent and £5 of that is for heating, you will only get a maximum of £40 Housing Benefit, as the charge for fuel will be deducted. If your weekly fuel charges are not stated as a separate amount, the council will deduct the amounts listed as follows:

81

Heating	£15.45
Hot water	£1.80
Cooking	£1.80
Lighting	£1.25
All fuel	£20.30

The amounts are lower if you occupy only one room.

2 Deductions for non-dependants living in your home

A deduction will normally be made from both your Housing Benefit and your Council Tax Benefit if you have someone else living with you who is not your partner or a dependent child nor a joint tenant or joint owner. This is because people such as grown-up sons and daughters (called 'non-dependants') are expected to contribute to housing costs. However, no deduction will be made if you or your partner are blind or receive Attendance Allowance or the care component of Disability Living Allowance. There are also some types of non-dependant who do not give rise to a deduction – for example, full-time students during term time.

If the person living with you is aged 18 or over, works 16 hours a week or more and does not receive Pension Credit and has a gross income of at least £116 a week, the rates of deduction are as follows:

Housing Benefit

Gross income of non-dependant	*Weekly deduction from rent*
£116.00 to £171.99	£17.00
£172.00 to £222.99	£23.35

£223.00 to £295.99	£38.20
£296.00 to £368.99	£43.50
£369 or more	£47.75

There will be no deduction from your Housing Benefit if the person who lives with you receives Pension Credit, or is under 25 and receives Income Support or income-based Jobseeker's Allowance (JSA). There will be a £7.40 deduction from your Housing Benefit for anyone else who is aged 18 or over and does not fall into any of the categories already mentioned.

Council Tax Benefit

Gross income of non-dependant	*Weekly deduction from Council Tax*
Gross income less than £172.00	£2.30
£172.00 to £295.99	£4.60
£296.00 to £368.99	£5.80
£369 or more	£6.95

Deductions are made from your Council Tax Benefit for non-dependants aged over 18 who normally live with you. There are four levels of deduction. If the non-dependant is working less than 16 hours per week, and is not receiving Pension Credit, the lowest deduction will apply. If the non-dependant is doing paid work for 16 hours or more a week, the level of deduction will depend on the non-dependant's gross weekly income.

For Council Tax Benefit there are some types of non-dependants who do not give rise to a deduction (such as full-time students). There is no deduction for a non-dependant receiving Pension Credit, Income Support or income-based JSA, while for others aged 18 or over not covered above there will be a £2.30 deduction.

Only one deduction is made for a non-dependent couple living with you.

A deduction may be delayed for 26 weeks if you or your partner are aged 65 or over and a non-dependant moves into your home, or the non-dependant's circumstances change to increase the deduction.

3 Your savings

Throughout this book the term 'savings' is used to cover savings, capital, investments and property.

If your savings are more than £16,000, you cannot normally get Housing Benefit or the main Council Tax Benefit. However, if you are receiving the guarantee part of the Pension Credit there is no savings limit. For a couple, savings are added together, but the limit is the same. You can have up to £6,000 in savings without it affecting your benefit.

If you are aged 60 or over and not receiving Pension Credit guarantee credit and have savings of between £6,000 and £16,000, an income of £1 a week for every £500 (or part of £500) over £6,000 will be taken into account in working out your benefit. For example, if you have savings of £7,480, you will be treated as having an income of £3 a week. Savings of £10,760 will be treated as £10 a week. This is called 'tariff income'. Savings of £6,000 or less will not affect your benefit.

If you are aged under 60 and have savings of between £6,000 and £16,000, an income of £1 a week for every £250 (or part of £250) over £6,000, will be taken into account in working out your benefit. For example, if you have savings of £6,300, you will be treated as having an income of £2 per week.

Savings and capital are normally valued at their current market or surrender value. If there are expenses involved in selling them, 10 per cent will be deducted. Most forms of savings and capital will be taken into account, including:

- cash;
- bank and building society accounts (including current accounts that do not pay interest);
- National Savings & Investments accounts and certificates (valued according to rules which the local authority will explain);
- premium bonds;
- income bonds;
- stocks and shares;
- property (other than your home); and
- a share of any savings you own jointly with other people – these will normally be divided equally by the number of joint owners to calculate your share (get advice if you need to value your share of jointly-owned property).

Some types of savings will be ignored, including:

- the value of your home if you own it and are living there;
- the surrender value of a life assurance policy (although if a policy is cashed in the money you receive will normally be counted);

85

- arrears of certain benefits, such as Attendance Allowance, Disability Living Allowance or Income Support, for 52 weeks from the date you receive them (or longer if the arrears are £5,000 or over and due to an official error);

- a lump-sum payment received because you deferred drawing your State Pension;

- your personal possessions; and

- the £10,000 ex-gratia payment for Far Eastern Prisoners of War (see page 135).

There are also other forms of savings not listed here which are ignored and there are circumstances when property or savings will not be taken into account for a certain period of time – contact the council or an advice agency for more information.

Deprivation of capital (notional capital) If you 'deprive' yourself of savings in order to get benefit or to increase the amount of benefit, you will be treated as still having those savings. This is known as 'notional capital'. This might occur if you give money to your family or buy expensive items in order to gain benefit. However, you will not be assessed as having notional capital if you have paid off debts or if your spending was 'reasonable' in your circumstances. You should seek advice if you are refused benefit because of notional capital.

4 Your income

This section lists the main types of income that are counted and the main types of income, or parts of income, that are ignored when working out Housing and Council Tax Benefit for people aged 60 and over. If you have any income from other sources you will need to check whether or not they are included. Income is assessed after tax and NI contributions have been paid. For a couple, the income of both partners is added together.

Income that is taken into account includes:

- State Pensions;

- occupational and personal pensions;

- the savings credit part of Pension Credit if you are not receiving the guarantee credit;

- income from annuities;

- most social security benefits (but see below for some exceptions);

- earnings (but see below for amounts ignored);

- Working Tax Credit;

- income from boarders or sub-tenants (but see below for parts ignored);

- regular payments from equity release schemes;

- maintenance payments from a spouse or former spouse; and

- assumed income from savings over £6,000.

Income that will be fully ignored includes:

- Pension Credit guarantee credit;

- Attendance Allowance;

- Disability Living Allowance;

- actual interest or income from savings or capital of £16,000 or less (only tariff income will be counted, as explained above). Interest is not counted as income but once it is paid into an account it will be counted as part of your savings;

- the special War Widow's Pension for 'pre-1973 widows', which is now £73.64 (in addition to the £10 of a War Widow/Widower's Pension outlined below); and

- voluntary or charitable payments – for example, money given to you by a charity, family or friends.

The following are examples of parts of weekly income that will also be ignored:

- £5 of your earnings if you work and are single;

- £10 of your or your partner's earnings from work;

- £20 of earnings if you work and you are a carer receiving the carer premium or in certain circumstances when you or your partner is disabled (instead of the £5 or £10 listed above);

- £10 of a War Widow/Widower's Pension or War Disablement Pension (the local authority has the discretion to increase the amount from these pensions that is ignored when working out your benefit, but not all authorities operate such schemes: contact your local authority for more information); and

- £20 of any payment from a sub-tenant or boarder and, in the case of a boarder, half of any payment over £20.

To work out your benefit, decide what kinds of income will be ignored and add up the remainder (including tariff income for savings between £6,000 and £16,000).

5 Your applicable amount

This is the weekly amount that is compared with your income to calculate your Housing and Council Tax Benefit. If your income is higher than this, you may still get some help with rent and the Council Tax. The basic personal allowances for people aged 60 or over are:

Single person aged 60–64	£124.05
Couple, one or both 60–64, both under 65	£189.35
Single person aged 65 or over	£143.80
Couple, one or both aged 65 or over	£215.50

In addition to these basic amounts some people will be entitled to a severe disability premium or a carer premium (or sometimes both). The rules for these are the same as for the additions in Pension Credit and are described on pages 58–61.

For people aged 60–64 the applicable amount is the same as the 'appropriate amount' in Pension Credit. For people aged 65 and over the amount is higher. This was to ensure that at the point of change from Income Support to Pension Credit everyone gained the full amount of savings credit and no-one lost Housing Benefit or Council Tax Benefit. However, if you are already receiving the higher levels of Housing Benefit and/or Council Tax Benefit for people aged 65 and over and you apply for Pension Credit, if you are not entitled to guarantee credit, the savings credit will be taken into account and will reduce your benefit. Even if your benefit is reduced, you will still be better off because your overall weekly income will increase.

6 Calculating Housing Benefit and Council Tax Benefit

Once you have worked out your applicable amount, compare this figure with your income, including any tariff income from savings over £6,000. If your income is the same as or less than your applicable amount, you will normally get all your rent and Council Tax paid (unless, for example, there are deductions for ineligible service charges, for other people living in your home or because your rent is considered too high). If you are not already receiving Pension Credit, then you may be entitled to it, so you should consider applying.

If your income is more than your applicable amount, the maximum benefit you can get is reduced. You first work out the difference between your income and your applicable amount. The maximum Housing Benefit payable is reduced by 65 per cent of this difference. The maximum Council Tax Benefit is reduced by 20 per cent of the difference.

Another way of explaining the calculation is to say that your maximum Housing Benefit is reduced by 65p for every pound that your income is more than your applicable amount. Your maximum Council Tax Benefit is reduced by 20p for every pound that your income is more than your applicable amount.

Example

Julie Walker is aged 64 and lives alone. Her income consists of a State Pension (Basic and Additional Pension) of £94 a week. She has £2,000 savings and pays £50 a week in rent and £14 a week in Council Tax (after the 25 per cent discount because she lives alone).

The maximum Housing Benefit she can get is £50 a week (100 per cent of her rent). The maximum Council Tax Benefit she can get is £14 a week (100 per cent of her Council Tax). There are no deductions for non-dependants because she lives alone.

Her savings will not affect her benefit as they are less than £6,000.

Julie's applicable amount is the standard personal allowance for someone aged 60–64 (£124.05).

Her income is less than her applicable amount, so she will get the maximum Housing Benefit of £50 a week for rent and the maximum Council Tax Benefit of £14 a week. She will also qualify for Pension Credit guarantee credit and should make a claim.

Example

Amir and Samina Khan are both aged 68 and live in a rented house. Amir receives Attendance Allowance and Samina cares for him. She applied for Carer's Allowance and although she satisfied the caring conditions she cannot be paid it because she is receiving a State Pension worth more than the allowance. However, this means that she has an 'underlying entitlement' to Carer's Allowance, so they qualify for the carer premium.

They pay £58 a week in rent. Their Council Tax is £16 a week. They have State Pensions of £160 a week between them, Amir's occupational pension of £95.96 a week, Pension Credit savings credit of £5.79 a week and savings of £11,700.

The maximum Housing Benefit they can get is £58. The maximum Council Tax Benefit they can get is £16. They have nobody else living with them, so there will be no deductions for non-dependants.

Amir and Samina add up their income

State Pension	£160.00
Occupational pension	£95.96
Tariff income (for savings over £6,000)	£12.00
Pension Credit savings credit	£5.79
Total	£273.75

They calculate their applicable amount

Personal allowance	£215.50
Carer premium	£27.75
Total	£243.25

Their income is more than their applicable amount, the difference being £30.50 (£273.75 – £243.25).

Their weekly benefit is worked out in the following way:

Rent

100% of rent	£58.00
Less 65% of difference	
(65% of £30.50)	£19.83
Housing Benefit	£38.17

Council Tax

100% of tax	£16.00
Less 20% of difference	
(20% of £30.50)	£6.10
Council Tax Benefit	£9.90

Total benefit is

Housing Benefit   £38.17

Council Tax Benefit   £9.90

Amir and Samina will have to pay £19.83 a week for rent and £6.10 towards the Council Tax.

Example

George and Anne Jones are both 78 and own their home. Their Council Tax is £20 a week. Their weekly income consists of State Pensions of £145.80 a week, income from an annuity of £46, and £67.70 from an occupational pension. They also have £14,000 savings.

They have never claimed benefits before but were worried because they were having to use their savings to pay their Council Tax bill. They asked their local advice agency about Pension Credit. It was explained that at present they would not be entitled to Pension Credit but they were advised to claim Council Tax Benefit. The maximum Council Tax Benefit they can get is £20. They have nobody else living with them, so there will be no deductions for non-dependants.

George and Anne add up their income

State Pension	£145.80
Occupational pension	£67.70
Annuity income	£46.00
Tariff income from savings	£16.00
Total	£275.50

Their applicable amount is the basic personal allowance for a couple aged over 65 (£215.50).

Their income is £60 more than their applicable amount.

Their weekly benefit is worked out in the following way:

Council Tax

100% of tax	£20.00
Less 20% of difference	
(20% of £60.00)	£12.00
Council Tax Benefit	£8.00

George and Anne will receive £8 a week (£416 over the year) towards their Council Tax.

If their granddaughter, who is aged 25 and earning £200 a week, comes to live with them, she will be counted as a 'non-dependant' and their benefit will be reduced by £4.60 a week.

Second adult rebate

If you are solely liable to pay the Council Tax, you might get a second adult rebate if one or more people with a low income live with you, regardless of the level of your savings and income. This will usually apply only to people who do not have a partner.

You may get a 25 per cent rebate if you are responsible for the Council Tax and you have one or more people receiving Pension Credit, Income Support or income-based Jobseeker's Allowance (JSA) living with you. A 15 per cent rebate is given if the person or people living with you have a joint gross income of less than £169; there is a 7.5 per cent rebate if their income is between £169 and £219.99. In assessing the income of people living with you, no account is taken of Attendance Allowance, Disability Living Allowance or the income of anyone receiving Pension Credit, Income Support or income-based JSA.

Example

Janice Grant is a widow who owns her own home. Her son is living with her and receives income-based JSA. Her Council Tax bill for the year is £800. She is not entitled to the main Council Tax Benefit because she has £18,000 savings. However, she applies for a rebate and receives the second adult rebate of 25 per cent (£200) because her son receives income-based JSA.

Some people will be entitled to the main Council Tax Benefit and the second adult rebate. In this case the local authority will award you whichever benefit will give you the greater amount.

Only brief details have been given here as this system can be complicated, so contact the council or a local advice agency if you need further information.

Benefit for people in different circumstances

Absence from home If you go into hospital on a temporary basis, you can continue to get Housing Benefit and Council Tax Benefit for up to 52 weeks (provided that you intend to return home). If you are temporarily away from home for other reasons, benefit will be paid for up to 13 weeks or up to 52 weeks depending on the reason for your absence. Contact the council or a local advice agency if you need more information about this. You cannot get benefit if you sub-let your home while you are away.

Benefit for two homes You can normally only get Housing Benefit for one home. However, there are some circumstances in which payments may be made for two homes. For example, you may qualify for benefit on two homes for up to four weeks if you have moved to a new home and it is reasonable that you could not avoid liability to make payments for both homes. Another example is where your move to a new home has been delayed because it was being adapted to meet disability needs. Entitlement to Housing Benefit for two homes is not automatic, so ask your local authority whether you qualify.

Council Tax Benefit is payable only for the home in which you normally live. It is not payable for second homes.

Discretionary housing payments You can apply to the local authority for an extra payment towards your rent and Council Tax if you are having difficulty meeting your bills. Your local authority will tell you how to make a claim and you will be able to give reasons why you need additional support.

How to claim

If you are claiming Pension Credit, you should also be asked if you want to apply for Housing Benefit and Council Tax Benefit and then you will be given a short three-page form which will mean that you do not need to give much of the same information to both The Pension Service and the local authority. If you are claiming Pension Credit over the phone, the staff there will fill in the Housing Benefit and Council Tax Benefit claim form for you at the same time. At the time of writing you still need to sign the short Housing and Council Tax Benefit claim form, which is posted to you, and send it to your local authority. However, from October 2008 The Pension Service will be able to forward all the information about your claim directly to the local authority so they can work out your Housing and Council Tax Benefit without you having to sign and return a form.

If you are not claiming Pension Credit, you claim Housing Benefit and Council Tax Benefit directly from your local authority (council). Before the local authority can work out how much to pay, it may require evidence such as details of your income, savings and the amount of rent you pay.

If you are a couple, only one of you should claim for benefit – it does not matter if the bill is sent in joint names or just to one of you. Your benefit will be calculated on the basis of your combined income and savings.

Backdating At the time of writing, Housing Benefit and Council Tax Benefit can be backdated for up to 52 weeks, as long as you have satisfied the conditions during that time. However, the Government has stated that it will reduce this period – from October 2008 claims will only be backdated for up to three months. Claim as soon as you think you might qualify so that you don't miss out on any benefit you are entitled to.

If your circumstances change If you are not receiving Pension Credit, you must report any changes that might affect your benefit to the local authority. If you are receiving Pension Credit, then whether you need to tell the local authority about changes will depend on the nature of the change and which part of Pension Credit you are receiving. For example, if you are receiving Pension Credit guarantee credit, then you will not need to report changes in your income and savings to the local authority. You may need to report these changes to

97

The Pension Service depending on whether or not you have an assessed income period (see pages 74–75).

If you are receiving the savings credit but not the guarantee credit, then there are some changes you must tell the local authority about. These include an increase in your savings to over £16,000, regardless of whether or not you have a Pension Credit assessed income period.

Your local authority will give you information about when you need to let it know if your circumstances change. If you are unsure, contact the local authority to check or otherwise you could have to repay money you have been overpaid or receive less benefit than you are entitled to.

Delays and administrative problems The local authority should let you know within 14 days of your claim whether you qualify for help (as long as you have provided any information and evidence needed). However, this sometimes takes much longer. If you are suffering hardship because the local authority has not yet worked out your claim for benefit or you are having problems with your benefit, contact Citizens Advice or a local advice centre for help.

How it is paid

For council tenants, Housing Benefit is usually paid by reducing the rent. If you are a private or housing association tenant, your Housing Benefit may be paid to you by cheque or into a bank account or direct to your landlord.

Most people will pay the Council Tax direct to their local authority, so when you claim benefit your bill will be reduced accordingly. Where this is not possible because, for example, you have already paid the whole bill, the local authority may send you a refund or credit your account.

Overpayment If you are paid too much benefit, this is known as an overpayment and in most circumstances the local authority can ask you to repay this money. However, an overpayment cannot normally be recovered if it was caused by an 'official error' and you could not reasonably be expected to have known you were being overpaid at the time. Even if the local authority can recover the benefit, it does have some discretion about whether to do so. It is a good idea to seek further advice if you are being asked to repay benefit.

If you disagree with a decision

If you disagree with a decision about your Housing Benefit or Council Tax Benefit, you can ask for the decision to be revised or appeal to an independent tribunal (see pages 41–45).

THE SOCIAL FUND

The Social Fund provides lump-sum payments for expenses which are difficult to meet from low income. There are Funeral Payments, which are described on pages 193–195, and Cold Weather Payments, which are explained on page 169. In addition there are Winter Fuel Payments which are not related to income (see pages 167–169). If you have other expenses – for example if you need a cooker or bedding – you may get help from the discretionary Social Fund in the form of Community Care Grants, Budgeting Loans or Crisis Loans, which are covered in this section.

The payments described here are different from most other social security benefits in that they are discretionary, and Budgeting Loans and Crisis Loans have to be repaid. There is a limited budget for the discretionary Social Fund, which restricts the overall amount that can be awarded in grants and loans in any financial year. There is a legal framework for the system and Social Fund decision-makers have to follow legal rules called 'directions' and take account of guidance which helps them make decisions. For Community Care Grants and Crisis Loans they must consider all the individual circumstances of the people who apply and decide which applications can be met from the budget. Awards of Budgeting Loans are more 'fact-based', as explained below, rather than being wholly discretionary, but they must still be made from a fixed budget.

Community Care Grants

These are available to people receiving Pension Credit, Income Support and income-based Jobseeker's Allowance, and to people who will be discharged from care within six weeks and are likely to receive these benefits on discharge. The grants do not have to be repaid. The amount of any savings you have over £1,000 (£500 for people under 60) will be deducted from any grant awarded. For example, if you have £1,100 savings and you need an item costing £300 you would only receive a grant for £200. If you are not sure whether you will get help, you have nothing to lose by applying. It is important to include all the relevant information (see below on 'How to apply').

Grants are available for certain purposes including:

- help with moving out of institutional or residential care (for example for a bed, a cooker, fuel connection or removal costs);

- help to enable you to remain living at home (for example for minor house repairs, bedding and essential furniture or removal costs to more suitable accommodation);

- help with exceptional pressures on families (for example caused by disability, chronic sickness or a breakdown in a relationship); and

- help with certain travel expenses (for example for visiting someone who is ill or attending a relative's funeral).

FOR MORE INFORMATION, see Jobcentre Plus leaflet SFLA5JP Grants and Loans from the Social Fund or detailed guide SB16 A Guide to the Social Fund (which is only available online).

Budgeting Loans

These are available to people who have been receiving Pension Credit, Income Support or income-based Jobseeker's Allowance for at least 26 weeks. They enable people to spread the cost of one-off expenses over a longer period. The loans, which are interest-free, have to be repaid, and the amount of any savings over £2,000 (£1,000 for people under 60) will reduce the amount of the loan.

The applications for Budgeting Loans and Community Care Grants are separate. So consider whether you might qualify for a grant before applying for a Budgeting Loan. You may be able to get a Budgeting Loan for one of the following categories:

- furniture and household equipment;

- clothing and footwear;

- removal costs and/or rent in advance;

- home improvements, maintenance or home security measures;

- travel expenses;

- expenses associated with seeking or going back to work; or

- hire purchase (HP) and other debts (for expenses associated with the categories outlined).

In deciding whether you can be awarded a loan, the Social Fund decision-maker will look at the time you have been receiving benefit, the people in your household and any loans you have already had from the Social Fund.

Crisis Loans

These interest-free loans are available to anyone (not just people receiving benefits such as Pension Credit) who needs something urgently in an emergency or as a result of a disaster (such as fire or flood). The Social Fund decision-maker will take into account any family savings or income available to you. You may be able to get a loan, provided that this is the only way of preventing serious damage or risk to your health or safety or that of a member of your family.

Repayment of loans

Budgeting or Crisis Loans will be awarded only if the officer thinks you will be able to repay them. Loan repayments will normally be deducted from your benefit and have to be repaid within 104 weeks. In special circumstances the repayment period may be extended further.

The repayment rates will be fixed after taking into account your income and your existing commitments. In the case of Crisis Loans, repayments will not normally begin until after the period of crisis is over.

If you take out a further loan from the Social Fund whilst still repaying an earlier loan, repayment of the further loan will not begin until the original loan has been repaid.

The repayment of loans can be rescheduled if you are having difficulty paying the original rate of repayment. If you are having difficulties, contact your Jobcentre Plus office or The Pension Service to discuss the level of repayment.

How to apply

To get application forms for a Community Care Grant or a Budgeting Loan, or to apply for a Crisis Loan, contact Jobcentre Plus by visiting the website (www.jobcentre plus.gov.uk) or by phone, using the number in the local phone book.

When applying for a Community Care Grant or Crisis Loan, give as much information as possible about your circumstances and why you need help (for example health problems). If there is not enough room on the form, use a separate sheet.

A local advice agency or Citizens Advice may be able to help you with the application. You may also wish to include a letter of support from your GP or social worker.

If you are unhappy about a decision

Community Care Grants and loans from the Social Fund are discretionary payments. If you disagree with a decision, you cannot appeal to an appeal tribunal, but instead there is a special system of review. Any request for a review must be made in writing within 28 days of the decision. The first stage of review is at the local office, and you are given the chance to put your case to a Social Fund Reviewing Officer. This is usually done over the phone rather than in person. If you are still dissatisfied, you can take your case to the Independent Review Service where it will be considered by a Social Fund Inspector, who is independent of your local Jobcentre Plus office. A local advice agency may be able to help if you want to ask for a review.

FOR MORE INFORMATION, see Jobcentre Plus leaflet SFLA5JP Grants and Loans from the Social Fund *or detailed guide SB16 (which is only available on the website).*

Disability Benefits and Paying for Care

This part of *Your Rights* describes the main Department for Work and Pensions benefits available to people who are ill or disabled and those who look after them.

Disability Living Allowance and Attendance Allowance are intended to help with the extra costs associated with disability and illness, while other benefits, such as Incapacity Benefit and Carer's Allowance, are paid to people who are unable to work or who can work only to a limited extent because of illness or disability or because they are a carer.

There is also a section about paying for care – either in your own home or in a care home – which includes information about local authority charging procedures and financial support.

ATTENDANCE ALLOWANCE AND DISABILITY LIVING ALLOWANCE

Attendance Allowance and Disability Living Allowance (DLA) are intended to provide help towards the extra costs arising from physical or mental disability. Which one you claim depends on your age.

To qualify for DLA you must need help with personal care, or have difficulty walking, or both, and you must claim before your 65th birthday. If you are 65 or over and need help with personal care, you should claim Attendance Allowance instead.

This section covers first the conditions for Attendance Allowance and then the conditions for Disability Living Allowance; the third part gives information that applies to both allowances.

Attendance Allowance

This is a benefit for people aged 65 or over who need help with personal care, or need supervision by day, or someone to watch over them by night, because of physical or mental disability. It does not depend on National Insurance (NI) contributions, is not affected by savings or income (other than Constant Attendance Allowance), and is paid on top of other benefits or pensions. Attendance Allowance is not taxable.

There are two weekly rates:

Higher rate	£67.00
Lower rate	£44.85

Who qualifies for Attendance Allowance? To qualify for Attendance Allowance you must fulfil all the following conditions:

- You are aged 65 or older.

- You meet the day and/or night conditions described below.

- You must also normally have satisfied the disability conditions for at least six months, but there are 'special rules' for people who are terminally ill, as explained on pages 118–119.

You will receive the lower rate if you fulfil either the day or the night conditions. You will get the higher rate if you fulfil both day and night conditions. You can receive the allowance if you live alone or with other people and regardless of whether or not you receive any help from someone else – what matters is that you need help with personal care, supervision or watching over, not whether you are actually getting help. You do not have to spend the allowance on paying for care: it is up to you how you use it. However, your local authority may take it into account when assessing whether, and how much, you need to pay for any care services you have.

Day conditions You can get the allowance if you are so disabled that you require frequent help throughout the day with your normal 'bodily functions', such as eating, getting in or out of bed, going to the toilet or washing. 'Seeing' and 'hearing' are considered bodily functions. For example, if you are visually impaired and need guidance when walking or someone to read your mail, or if you are deaf and need help with communicating, this could help you satisfy the requirement for needing 'frequent help'. You can also get the allowance if you need continual supervision throughout the day to avoid putting yourself or others in substantial danger, or if you need someone with you when you are on renal dialysis.

Night conditions You can also get the allowance if you are so disabled that you require prolonged (generally periods of at least 20 minutes) or repeated (generally at least twice nightly) attention during the night to help you with your bodily functions – for example, going to the toilet and getting in and out of bed. You can also get the allowance if another person needs to be awake for a prolonged period or at frequent intervals at night in order to watch over you to avoid putting yourself or others in substantial danger.

The next section covers the qualifying conditions for Disability Living Allowance. You should turn to pages 114–120 for information that covers both allowances, such as how to make a claim and what happens if you are away from home.

Disability Living Allowance

This benefit is for people who make a claim before the age of 65, and who, because of their physical or mental disability:

- need help with personal care, or need supervision by day, or need someone to watch over them at night; or

- are unable to walk, have great difficulty walking, or need someone with them when walking in unfamiliar places outdoors; or

- need help with both of these.

Disability Living Allowance (DLA) does not depend on NI contributions, is not affected by savings or income (other than Constant Attendance Allowance or War

Pensioners' Mobility Supplement), and is paid on top of other benefits or pensions. DLA is not taxable.

There are two parts to DLA: the 'care component', which is paid at one of three rates; and the 'mobility component', which has two different levels. The weekly rates are:

DLA care component	*DLA mobility component*
Highest rate £67.00	Higher rate £46.75
Middle rate £44.85	Lower rate £17.75
Lowest rate £17.75	

Who qualifies for DLA? To qualify for DLA you must fulfil all the following conditions:

- You meet one or more of the care or mobility conditions described below.

- You are aged under 65 when you claim.

- You must also normally have satisfied the disability conditions for at least three months, and be expected to satisfy them for at least the next six months, but there are 'special rules' for people who are terminally ill, as explained on pages 118–119.

Although you must have become disabled, and made a claim, before the age of 65, once you are awarded the allowance it will continue, without an age limit, as long as you satisfy either the care or the mobility conditions. If you are receiving the lowest or middle rate of the care component and your care needs change, you may be able to qualify for a higher rate after six months. You cannot normally start to receive the lowest rate of the care component or the mobility component after the age of 65. However, you may be able to receive it if you are already getting one of the components and you can show that you met the conditions for the other component before the age of 65. Seek advice if you think that this may apply to you.

The care component The care component of DLA is for people who need help with personal care, supervision or watching over because of physical or mental illness or disability. It does not matter if you live alone or with other people, or whether or not you receive any help from someone else – what matters is that you need help with personal care, supervision or watching over, not whether you are actually getting help. You do not have to spend the allowance on paying for care: it is up to you how you use it. However, your local authority may take it into account when assessing whether, and how much, you need to pay for any care services you have.

You will receive £17.75 if you fulfil one of the lowest-rate conditions but not the day or night conditions described below. You will receive the middle rate if you fulfil either a day or a night condition. The highest rate is for those who fulfil both a day and a night condition. You will see that the day and night conditions are the same as those for Attendance Allowance.

Lowest-rate conditions
You will fulfil this condition if you need help with 'bodily functions' for a significant portion of the day, either at one single period or a number of times. For example, you might need some help to get up in the morning and go to bed in the evening but manage alone for the rest of the day. You will also fulfil this condition

if, as a result of your disability, you could not prepare a main cooked meal for yourself even if you had the ingredients.

Day conditions

You will fulfil this condition if you are so disabled that you require frequent help throughout the day with your normal bodily functions, such as eating, getting in or out of bed, going to the toilet or washing. 'Seeing' and 'hearing' are considered bodily functions. For example, if you are visually impaired and need guidance when walking or someone to read your mail, or you are deaf and need help with communicating, this could help you satisfy the requirement for needing 'frequent help'. You can also get the allowance if you need continual supervision throughout the day to avoid putting yourself or others in substantial danger, or if you need someone with you when you are on renal dialysis.

Night conditions

You will fulfil this condition if you are so disabled that you require prolonged (generally periods of at least 20 minutes) or repeated (generally at least twice nightly) attention during the night to help you with your bodily functions – for example, going to the toilet and getting in and out of bed. You can also get the allowance if another person needs to be awake for a prolonged period or at frequent intervals throughout the night in order to watch over you to avoid putting yourself or others in substantial danger.

The mobility component Although the mobility component is given to people who need help getting around, you can spend it how you choose. Remember that it is not available to people who become disabled, or make a claim, after the age of 65. Local authorities cannot take into account your mobility component when assessing whether, and how much, you need to pay for any care services you have.

You can receive the higher level if you are unable to walk or have great difficulty in walking without severe discomfort or seriously affecting your health because of a physical disability. The higher level is also available to people who are both 100 per cent disabled through blindness and 80 per cent disabled through deafness and need someone with them when outdoors, to all people who have lost both legs at or above the ankle (or were born without legs or feet), and to severely mentally disabled people who have severe behavioural problems and can get the highest rate of the care component. If you can walk but need someone with you for guidance or supervision when out of doors in unfamiliar places, you may be awarded the lower level.

Using a car

If you own a car and get the higher rate of the mobility component of DLA, you may not have to pay road tax. If someone drives a car for you, they can also apply for exemption from road tax. You will get details about this and about using your mobility component to get a car on contract hire or hire purchase through the Motability scheme when you first get the allowance (see page 208 for Motability's address).

You can also apply to your local authority for a blue badge (previously an orange badge), which allows parking with some limitations but without charge at meters or where waiting is restricted. Some local authorities make a small charge for issuing the badge.

Examples of people who may receive DLA

Ellen Johnson is 62 and cannot walk very far owing to severe osteo-arthritis in her hips and hands. Although she can manage to care for herself, she finds cooking very difficult because she cannot do tasks such as cutting, lifting and pouring. She applied for DLA and was awarded the higher level of the mobility component and the lowest rate of the care component.

Albert Brown is 64 and suffers from dementia. During the day his wife or another relative stays with him all the time because he is very forgetful and sometimes wanders off or turns on the gas without lighting it. He normally sleeps all through the night. His wife applied for DLA on his behalf and he was awarded the middle rate of the care component (because he needs supervision during the day) and the lower rate of the mobility component because he needs guidance and supervision when outdoors.

Sarah Bloom is 68 and had a severe stroke six months ago which left her unable to walk and needing a lot of help, for example with washing, dressing and eating. Because she is 68 she is too old to claim DLA. She cannot get any help with her mobility needs but she can apply for Attendance Allowance because she needs personal care.

Remember that these are just examples and your situation is probably different. Whether you qualify for DLA, and if so at what rate, will depend on your particular circumstances.

Rules covering both Attendance Allowance and Disability Living Allowance

If you are away from home If you are receiving NHS treatment in a hospital, you cannot start to receive Attendance Allowance or DLA (although you can make a claim and, if you fulfil the conditions, the allowance can be paid when you go home). However, you may receive either of these allowances if you are a private patient paying for the cost of hospital services.

If you are already receiving Attendance Allowance or DLA and you go into hospital, you will be able to continue to receive the allowance for up to four weeks. However, the allowance will stop sooner if your admission is within 28 days of a previous stay in hospital. The days you are admitted and discharged do not count as days in hospital.

If you have a current contract with Motability, there are special rules that can enable you to continue to receive payment of the mobility component while in hospital.

Before July 1996, a stay in hospital did not normally affect the mobility component of DLA. Some people in hospital for 12 months or more in July 1996 received transitional protection and can continue to get an amount equivalent to the lower rate of the mobility component.

For information about Attendance Allowance and DLA for people in care homes, see pages 151–152.

Living abroad In general you need to be normally resident in the UK and present here when you make your claim, and (unless you are applying under the special rules for terminally ill people) have been here or in the Isle of Man, or Jersey or Guernsey, for at least 26 weeks of the last 12 months. Time spent in another

114

European Economic Area (EEA) country may count in some cases.

In October 2007 there was a European ruling which could affect the payment of some disability benefits abroad. At the time of writing the implications of this ruling were being considered. If you are living in the EEA or Switzerland, or are intending to move there to live permanently, you may, in certain circumstances, be able to retain or claim Attendance Allowance or the care component of the Disability Living Allowance.

FOR MORE INFORMATION, look on the website at www.direct.gov.uk or write to Exportability Co-ordinator, Room B120D, Disability and Carers Service, Warbreck House, Warbreck Hill Road, Blackpool FY2 0YE, Tel: 08457 123456.

In general, a holiday abroad does not affect Attendance Allowance or DLA, nor do periods abroad for medical treatment. You should let your pension centre know when you intend to go abroad so that payment of the allowance while you are abroad can be considered.

How to claim You can get the claim form for Attendance Allowance (AA1) or DLA (DLA1):

- by telephoning the Benefit Enquiry Line on 0800 88 22 00 (Textphone: 0800 24 33 55);

- by sending off the tear-off slip on the leaflet *Attendance Allowance* or *Disability Living Allowance*;

- from some local advice agencies; or

- on the internet (at www.direct.gov.uk/en/ DisabledPeople).You can also claim online at that website.

115

If the forms are sent to you because you contacted the Benefit Enquiry Line, from a DWP office or because you returned the tear-off slip, they will be dated. As long as you return the form in the envelope provided within six weeks, your claim, if successful, will start on the day your request was received. If you get the claim pack from a local advice agency, unless it has been designated as an 'Alternative Office', this will not normally be dated and the claim will start from the date the form is received by the Disability and Carers Service.

The intention is that people can describe how their disability affects them on the form and that a medical examination will not normally be necessary. Although changes have been made to improve the forms, they are still quite long and you may want to have some assistance.

You can get help to fill in the form from a friend or relative or a local advice agency, or you can phone the Benefits Enquiry Line on Freephone 0800 88 22 00. If it is difficult for you to get out, you can ask for someone to visit to help you with the form.

FOR MORE INFORMATION, contact The Disability Alliance (address on page 207), which produces guides to help people claim Attendance Allowance and DLA.

If you have difficulty completing the claim form and would rather have a medical examination, you can ask for a doctor to visit. When filling in the form, remember that it does not matter if you actually receive any help or not. Be sure to say what activities are difficult or impossible for you to do. For example, you may have to get dressed on your own because there is no one to help you but do explain if it takes a long time or if it is difficult. If you feel that having answered the questions you have not given a good picture of how your disability affects you, add any extra information you think would be helpful. If you have any problems with filling in the form, do ask for help. There is also a space on the form for your doctor or someone else who knows about your circumstances to complete.

If your claim cannot be decided from the information in the form, the Disability and Carers Service may phone for more information, ask for further information from someone such as your doctor or community nurse, or it may arrange a medical examination.

If an appointment is made for a doctor to visit, you may want a friend or relative to be there at that time. This will be particularly important if you have difficulty making yourself understood. The doctor, who will not be your own doctor but one appointed by the DWP, will probably examine you and ask further questions. It may be useful to make a note beforehand of the things you need to tell the doctor about when you need help or the difficulties you experience.

When to claim Although you normally need to fulfil the qualifying conditions for three months before you can start getting DLA and six months for Attendance Allowance, if you have only recently become disabled you should still apply as it may take some weeks to deal with your claim.

If you are receiving a lower level of one of the allowances but your condition has deteriorated so you might now qualify for a higher level, you can ask for your case to be reconsidered. You will need to satisfy the

117

care or mobility conditions for the higher level for three months (DLA) or six months (Attendance Allowance) before it can be paid.

You should be aware that if you ask for your case to be looked at again, there is a possibility that instead of awarding a higher level your benefit might be stopped or reduced. You may want to seek help from a local advice agency to discuss your position and to ensure that you include all the relevant information if you ask for your benefit to be reconsidered.

Terminal illness People who are terminally ill can claim DLA or Attendance Allowance without the three-month or six-month waiting period under 'Special Rules' which make the application process quicker and simpler. They will be considered to be terminally ill if they have a progressive illness that is likely to limit their life expectancy to six months or less.

To claim, ask your doctor for a DS1500 report, which gives details of your condition. If you are sending the DS1500 report with the Attendance Allowance or DLA form, make sure that you have ticked the special rules box. You will not need to complete the whole form – information next to the special rules box explains which parts you need to fill in. Then sign the claim form and send it, and the DS1500, in the envelope provided.

If you are paid under the Special Rules, you will automatically receive the higher rate of Attendance Allowance or the highest level of the care component of DLA. However, if you are under the age of 65 and you want to claim the mobility component of DLA, you will need to fill in the mobility-related sections as part of your claim. Claims should be handled within 10 to 14 days and a medical examination will not normally be necessary.

If you are not sending the DS1500 report with your claim, you will need to complete all parts of the Attendance Allowance or DLA claim forms.

An application can be made by another person on behalf of someone who is terminally ill with or without their knowledge, so it is possible for people to receive an allowance under the Special Rules without knowing their prognosis.

Effect on other benefits Sometimes if you become entitled to Attendance Allowance or DLA this will also enable you to start receiving other benefits, such as Pension Credit, Housing Benefit or Council Tax Benefit, because these benefits can be higher if you are receiving a disability benefit. You will need to claim these benefits and may be able to receive payments backdated to the time your disability benefit started. If you are not sure of your position, get help from a local advice agency.

How it is paid Attendance Allowance or DLA may be awarded indefinitely or for a set period, in which case it will be reviewed at the end of this time. If your allowance is awarded for a fixed period, you should be sent a renewal claim before the end of that period. There is a system of periodic review for DLA which means that you may be sent a questionnaire or receive a visit to check if your needs are still the same.

Attendance Allowance is normally paid four-weekly in arrears directly into a bank, building society or other account. If payment into an account is not suitable for you, weekly cheques will be sent in the post (see pages 19–20 for more information). If you are receiving another benefit or pension, they will normally be paid together. DLA is normally paid four-weekly in arrears unless you were getting Attendance Allowance by weekly order book before April 1992. However, people claiming either Attendance Allowance or DLA under the Special Rules because they are terminally ill can get weekly payments in advance.

If you disagree with a decision If you disagree with a decision about your allowance, you can ask for the decision to be reviewed or make an appeal. You will be sent details about how to do this when you receive the decision. It is important to challenge a decision or get advice as quickly as possible because there are time limits for doing so which generally mean that you must take action within one month – see pages 41–45 for more information or look at the *Disability Rights Handbook* which has more detailed information (see page 211).

FOR MORE INFORMATION, see DWP leaflet Attendance Allowance *and claim form AA1, or for DLA, see DWP leaflet* Disability Living Allowance *and claim form DLA1.*

CARER'S ALLOWANCE

Carer's Allowance (which used to be called Invalid Care Allowance) is a benefit for people who are unable to work full-time because they are caring for a severely disabled person for at least 35 hours a week. The benefit is not dependent on having paid NI contributions. Carer's Allowance is taxable.

Do note that in some situations the person you care for could lose money if you start to receive Carer's Allowance. This will apply to a disabled person who receives the severe disability premium or addition as part of their Pension Credit, Income Support, Housing Benefit or Council Tax Benefit. (See pages 58–59 for more information about the severe disability premium/addition.)

The weekly rates are:

Carer	£50.55
Adult dependant	£30.20

The person being cared for must be receiving one of the allowances referred to below, such as Attendance Allowance. They do not have to be a relative and may live separately or with the carer.

Entitlement to Carer's Allowance may continue for up to eight weeks after the death of the person being cared for.

Who qualifies?

To qualify you must spend at least 35 hours a week looking after someone who is receiving Attendance Allowance (higher or lower rate), the care component of Disability Living Allowance (middle or highest rate), or Constant Attendance Allowance of £54.80 or more paid with an industrial, war or service pension.

There is no upper age limit for claiming Carer's Allowance, although if you are receiving a State Pension or another benefit you may not receive any or all of the allowance on top of this.

Claims can be made, with full backdating, up to three months after the disabled person who receives the care is

121

awarded Attendance Allowance, the middle or highest rate of the Disability Living Allowance care component, or a qualifying rate of Constant Attendance Allowance. Entitlement will start from the same date as the disabled person's entitlement, providing the qualifying conditions have been met throughout the period.

You cannot get Carer's Allowance if you earn more than £95 a week after the deduction of allowable expenses. This earnings limit increased in October 2007 when the minimum wage went up and so may change again during 2008. The extra £30.20 which can be claimed for a dependent adult will not be paid if that person earns more than £30.20 a week, including any occupational or personal pension. It also may not be paid if they are receiving a State Pension or certain other benefits. When calculating the net earnings of the carer or their partner, certain work expenses are deducted.

Overlap with the State Pension and increases to other benefits

If you are already getting £50.55 a week or more from certain other social security benefits or pensions, you may not be able to get Carer's Allowance as well. This is because it 'overlaps' with some benefits, including Incapacity Benefit, State Pension and Widow's Pension. If you have a spouse, civil partner or partner who is claiming an addition to their benefit for you, that addition will be reduced by the amount of Carer's Allowance received.

However, if you have a low income it may still be worth claiming Carer's Allowance even though it may not be paid in addition to your present benefit or pension. Although Carer's Allowance is counted as income if you claim Pension Credit, Income Support, Housing Benefit or Council Tax Benefit, people entitled to Carer's Allowance may be able to get higher rates of these benefits, owing to the 'carer premium' (carer addition in Pension Credit).

Example

Olive Zhukova is 62 and looks after her mother who gets Attendance Allowance. Olive has no savings and has a total income of £130.70 (State Pension of £90.70 and an occupational pension of £40 a week). She is not entitled to Pension Credit because her income is more than £124.05 – the basic Pension Credit level for someone over 60.

She applies for Carer's Allowance but, although she satisfies the conditions, it cannot be paid because her State Pension is more than £50.55 – the level of the allowance. However, because she is entitled to Carer's Allowance her Pension Credit rate is now £151.80 – the basic rate of £124.05 plus the carer addition of £27.75. She is now entitled to £21.10 in Pension Credit to bring her pensions of £130.70 up to the Pension Credit rate.

Protecting your pension

If you are entitled to Carer's Allowance, NI contributions will be automatically credited to protect your right to a future State Pension, unless you have retained the right to pay the married woman's reduced-rate contributions. If you receive another benefit instead and are not working regularly because you are caring for someone, you may get Home Responsibilities Protection (see pages 16–18). Entitlement to Carer's Allowance can also help you build up State Second Pension, as explained on page 23.

123

Carer's Allowance after State Pension age

If you are receiving Carer's Allowance when you reach State Pension age (currently 60 for women born on or before 5 April 1950, 65 for men), it will be adjusted to take account of any State Pension you draw. If your State Pension is £50.55 or more, payment of Carer's Allowance will stop. If your State Pension is less than £50.55, the Carer's Allowance will be reduced by the amount of the State Pension received. If you are not entitled to a State Pension or do not claim one, Carer's Allowance may continue.

If you were 65 or over on 28 October 2002 and receiving Invalid Care Allowance when the upper age limit for claiming was abolished, you may be able to continue to receive Carer's Allowance even if you are no longer caring. Otherwise the allowance will stop when you are no longer caring or up to eight weeks later if the person you care for dies.

How to claim

To make a claim you will need claim pack DS700, or DS700(SP) if you receive a State Pension. You can get these packs from your local Jobcentre Plus office, by ringing the Benefit Enquiry Line on Freephone 0800 88 22 00 or the Carer's Allowance claim pack order line on 01772 899729 (Textphone: 01772 562202), or on the internet (www.direct.gov.uk) where you can also claim online.

FOR MORE INFORMATION, see DWP leaflet CAA5DCS Carer's Allowance. *Carers UK produces information for carers – see page 206 for the address.*

STATUTORY SICK PAY

If you are an employee earning at least £90 a week, you will probably be entitled to Statutory Sick Pay (SSP) if you are off sick for at least four days in a row. There is no upper age limit. SSP can continue for up to 28 weeks and it will be paid by your employer. The weekly rate is £75.40. You may also get sick pay from your employer's own scheme, depending on the terms and conditions. SSP is taxable. Contact your employer for details.

If you are unable to work because of sickness but not entitled to SSP, for example because you are self-employed or unemployed, you may be entitled to Incapacity Benefit, as explained below.

INCAPACITY BENEFIT

This is a benefit for people who are unable to work owing to illness or disability. It is based on NI contributions (except for some people disabled early in life). It is not generally means tested but for claims on or after 6 April 2001 a personal or occupational pension of more than £85 a week may reduce benefit, as explained below.

Legislation has been agreed by Parliament to replace Incapacity Benefit (and Income Support paid on the grounds of ill health) with a new benefit called Employment and Support Allowance, which will have contributory and means-tested elements. This will apply to new claimants when it is introduced, which is expected to be Autumn 2008.

FOR MORE INFORMATION, see the Disability Rights Handbook *(see page 211). The Spring 2008 edition will include a summary of the scheme and a supplement will be produced later in the year with*

125

more detailed information. There will also be information on the Jobcentre Plus website (www.jobcentreplus.gov.uk).

This section mainly covers the current rules for Incapacity Benefit, but gives brief information on page 131 about the transitional rules for people who were transferred from Invalidity Benefit to Incapacity Benefit in April 1995.

There are three levels of Incapacity Benefit. If you are an employee, you will probably be paid Statutory Sick Pay (SSP) by your employer for the first 28 weeks that you are unable to work (see above). However, if you are not entitled to SSP, for example because you are self-employed or unemployed, you may be able to get the short-term lower rate of Incapacity Benefit for up to 28 weeks. The short-term higher rate of Incapacity Benefit is paid from 29 weeks to 52 weeks of incapacity, while the long-term rate is paid from week 53. (People who are terminally ill or who receive the highest rate of the care component of Disability Living Allowance (DLA) will receive the long-term rate from 29 weeks.) The long-term rate can continue up to State Pension age as long as you remain unable to work. The short-term higher rate and the long-term rate are taxable, but the short-term lower rate is not.

The weekly rates of Incapacity Benefit are:

Short-term lower rate (under State Pension age)	£63.75
Short-term higher rate (under State Pension age)	£75.40
Long-term rate	£84.50

If you become unable to work before the age of 45, you will receive an age addition which will be paid when you start to receive the long-term rate of Incapacity Benefit. There are two rates, depending on the age at which you become unable to work:

Under 35	£17.75
35–44	£8.90

Who qualifies?

To qualify for Incapacity Benefit you must be incapable of work and be under State Pension age (currently 60 for women born on or before 5 April 1950, 65 for men) when your period of incapacity began.

You must normally also satisfy certain NI contribution conditions in the last three tax years; or there are youth provisions for certain people disabled before the age of 20 (25 for people in education or training before age 20).

The incapacity tests The 'own occupation test' applies if you have been in a regular occupation for at least 16 hours a week for more than 8 weeks out of the last 21 weeks before you became incapable of work. For the first 28 weeks of incapacity you will normally only need to provide a medical certificate from your doctor stating that you are unable to do your normal job, if you have one. In some circumstances, a doctor working on behalf of the DWP may also be asked for advice.

After 28 weeks, or from the start of incapacity if you have not worked for 8 out of the 21 weeks before your claim, most people will have to undertake a 'personal capability assessment'. This will involve a questionnaire and, in some cases, a medical examination, to assess your ability to carry out specific everyday activities.

These relate to physical, sensory and mental functions, and include activities such as walking, climbing stairs, lifting and carrying, and hearing and vision. These assessment processes can begin earlier than the 28th week. However, you will not be subject to the incapacity test if you are terminally ill, receive the highest care component of DLA, are registered blind, have certain severe medical conditions, or in some circumstances when you are entitled to Industrial Injuries Disablement Benefit or a War Pension.

Increases for a husband, wife or civil partner You may be able to get increased Incapacity Benefit for your husband, wife or civil partner, or for a person who looks after your children or qualifying young persons. You may be entitled to an increase for an adult dependant if your husband, wife or civil partner is aged 60 or over. If you are receiving the long-term rate of Incapacity Benefit, the increase for a dependant is £50.55 a week. If you are receiving either of the short-term rates, and you are under State Pension age, the increase is £39.40.

However, these increases 'overlap' with any State Pension or certain other State benefits that your dependant is receiving. So if, for example, you are a married man and your wife had a State Pension of £60 a week, you would not be entitled to an increase for her. If her State Pension was £25 a week, the amount you could receive would be reduced by £25.

If your spouse or civil partner has earnings of more than £60.50 a week (if you are getting the long-term rate) or £39.40 a week (for the short-term rate), then you cannot receive an adult dependency increase – any occupational or personal pension your spouse/civil partner receives will be counted as earnings.

Work and Incapacity Benefit Under the 'permitted work' rules you are able to work for up to 16 hours a week and earn up to £88.50 a week for up to 52 weeks. (This figure of £88.50 may increase in October 2008 if the minimum wage rises.) After this period most people can only work and earn up to £20 a week. However, you will be able to continue to earn up to £88.50 a week if you are in certain types of 'supported permitted work', such as work in a sheltered workshop, or if you are someone who is exempt from the personal capability assessment (see above). You must tell the DWP that you are working. For more information contact your Jobcentre Plus office.

Occupational and personal pensions If you make a claim for Incapacity Benefit and you have an occupational, stakeholder or personal pension of more than £85 a week, this will normally reduce your benefit. For every £1 of pension more than £85, you will lose 50 pence of benefit.

A pension will not reduce your benefit if you have been receiving Incapacity Benefit since before 6 April 2001, nor do these rules apply to new claimants in receipt of the highest rate of the care component of Disability Living Allowance.

When you reach State Pension age

The long-term rate of Incapacity Benefit cannot be paid after State Pension age. So once you reach State Pension age (currently 60 for women born on or before 5 April 1950, 65 for men), you should draw the State Pension. It will be worked out as explained in the section starting on page 2, although if you were receiving an age addition with your Incapacity Benefit this can be paid

129

with your State Pension as an invalidity addition (after the deduction of any Additional State Pension and contracted-out deductions).

If you become incapable of work before State Pension age and are receiving short-term Incapacity Benefit, this can continue until you have been unable to work for up to a year. For people over State Pension age the short-term lower rate of Incapacity Benefit is £81.10 a week and the higher rate is £84.50, although you may get less if you do not have enough contributions for a full Basic State Pension. You may also receive Additional State Pension and Graduated Retirement Benefit. There is an adult dependency increase of £48.65 which you may receive if your husband, wife or civil partner is aged 60 or over – depending on any earnings, pensions or other benefits they receive.

How to claim

To claim Incapacity Benefit, contact your local Jobcentre Plus office. People claiming Incapacity Benefit (and other benefits for people of working age) will normally be required to attend a work-focussed interview as a condition of benefit. The aim is to look at work options, as well as to provide information about what practical and financial help is available. Schemes under the 'Pathways to Work' programme are running in some areas which provide additional support and are gradually being introduced nationally.

If you disagree with a decision

If you disagree with a decision about your benefit, you can ask for the decision to be revised or you can make an appeal, as explained on pages 41–45.

If you were receiving Invalidity Benefit on 12 April 1995

If you were transferred from Invalidity Benefit to Incapacity Benefit in April 1995 and have continued to receive Incapacity Benefit since then (without a break of more than eight weeks, or longer if covered by certain linking rules), you will be covered by the transitional rules, which are explained briefly here. Under the transitional rules, your Incapacity Benefit will not be taxable and some people will be exempt from the personal capability assessment.

The basic rate of Incapacity Benefit is £84.50 (which is the same as the long-term rate for new claimants) and the increase for a dependent husband or wife is also the same (£50.55), although if you were receiving an increase for a dependent husband or wife with your Invalidity Benefit, this can continue to be paid if your spouse is under 60.

You may receive Invalidity Allowance if you were previously getting it with your Invalidity Benefit. The rates, which depend on the age at which you became unable to work, are:

Under 40	£17.75
40–49	£11.40
Men 50–59, women 50–54	£5.70

Some people also receive an Additional Rate based on any entitlement to Additional State Pension built up between 1978 and 1991. This is paid at a frozen amount and 'overlaps' with Invalidity Allowance. In other respects the Incapacity Benefit rules are generally the same as for new claimants and are described on page 125.

131

SEVERE DISABLEMENT ALLOWANCE

Severe Disablement Allowance (SDA) was abolished for new claimants on 6 April 2001. However, you can still receive it if you were entitled to the benefit on or before 5 April 2001 and have been receiving it continuously since then (although short breaks may be covered by certain linking rules). If you are already in receipt of SDA it can be paid as long as you continue to satisfy the entitlement conditions. It is a benefit for people who are incapable of working but who do not have enough contributions to get Incapacity Benefit.

If you are under State Pension age and become unable to work now due to ill health, you may be able to claim Incapacity Benefit if you fulfil the contribution conditions; otherwise you may be entitled to help through income-related benefits.

SDA is not based on NI contributions and is not taxable. The basic weekly rates are:

Claimant	£51.05
Adult dependant	£30.40

There are also additions for people who became unable to work before the age of 60; these are added to the basic rate of £51.05. The weekly rates are:

Under 40	£17.75
40–49	£11.40
50–59	£5.70

SDA is not means-tested but is taken into account if you apply for income-related benefits such as Income Support or Pension Credit. Contact a local advice agency or write to Age Concern at the address on page 222 if you need more information about SDA.

If you applied on or after 13 April 1995, you will only have received the adult dependency increase for your husband or wife if they are aged 60 or over. This now also applies to civil partners. If they have earnings over £60.50 or receive a State Pension or benefit of £30.40 or over, you may not be able to get this increase. If you have been receiving the increase since before 13 April 1995, it can continue, even if your husband or wife is under 60.

SDA can continue to be paid after you reach State Pension age but the 'overlapping benefit' rules apply, which means that it is not paid in addition to certain other State Pensions or benefits. You cannot receive both the full amount of SDA and a State Pension. If you do not qualify for a State Pension or it is less than SDA, you can continue to receive SDA to make your benefit up to the basic level of £51.05 plus the age addition if you qualify for one. You can continue to receive SDA instead of drawing your State Pension.

OTHER BENEFITS FOR PEOPLE WITH DISABILITIES

This section gives brief information about other benefits for people with disabilities. More detailed information is given in the leaflets mentioned or you could look at the *Disability Rights Handbook* (see page 211).

Industrial injuries scheme

The industrial injuries scheme can provide help to people who are disabled as a result of an accident at work or an industrial disease.

The main benefit is Disablement Benefit, which can be paid in addition to other National Insurance benefits such as Incapacity Benefit/Employment and Support Allowance or State Pension. The level of payment depends on how disabled you are assessed as being.

If you are awarded Disablement Benefit at the 100 per cent rate, you may also qualify for Constant Attendance Allowance if you need care and attention. There is also an Exceptionally Severe Disablement Allowance for those who are likely to need high levels of attention on a permanent basis.

FOR MORE INFORMATION, see leaflet DWP1004 Industrial Injuries Disablement Benefits: Help if you're Ill or Disabled because of your Job.

War Pensions

You may be entitled to some financial help if you are disabled (physically or mentally) or widowed as a result of service in the UK Armed Forces. You may get a tax-free lump sum or a pension. Civilians may also be entitled to financial help in some circumstances.

If you need care and attention because of your pensioned disablement you may also receive Constant Attendance Allowance and a Mobility Supplement if you have difficulty walking.

FOR MORE INFORMATION about war pensions, ring the Veterans Helpline on Freephone 0800 169 2277. You can also ask for details of your nearest War Pensioner's Welfare Service. This is an advice and support service for all war pensioners and war widows/widowers/surviving civil partners living in the UK. The Welfare Service also gives advice and assistance to anyone who has served in the UK Armed Forces.

Ex-gratia payments for British groups held prisoner by the Japanese Some British people (and in some cases their widows or widowers) who were held prisoner by the Japanese in the Second World War are entitled to a single ex-gratia payment of £10,000. These payments are not taken into account for income-related benefits.

FOR MORE INFORMATION, contact the Service Personnel and Veterans Agency on Freephone 0800 169 2277.

PAYING FOR CARE

This section explains the help you can get with paying for the costs of care in all settings. This might be care at home (such as personal care or domestic help in your home, day care or a night sitting service) or care in a care home. It covers people living in England, Scotland and Wales. Although the system in Northern Ireland is broadly similar, there are some differences, so contact Age Concern Northern Ireland at the address on page 222 if you need more information.

Many people buy their own care without social services' help. This section looks at the help you can receive from social services and how you may be charged for that help. There are national rules for charging for care in care homes but each local authority is able to decide whether and how much to charge for care to help you remain at home, subject to certain minimum requirements.

Applying for help with care

If you need help with your care, either to help you to remain at home or if you think you might need to move into a care home, you can ask for an assessment of

135

your needs by the local authority (the county, metropolitan or London Borough or unitary authority). The social services department (social work department in Scotland) will be responsible for arranging an assessment of your care needs.

After this assessment it will decide whether it can offer you any help either to enable you to stay at home or in a care home. Each local authority has its own criteria for making these decisions within a national framework. Some local authorities have a ceiling on the amount of care (either the number of hours or the cost) they will provide to help you remain at home. If you do not agree with the decision, you can make a complaint through the complaints procedure.

In England and Wales your carer (if you have one) is entitled to an assessment in their own right and to services that will help them care for you. They have a right to an assessment of their needs even if you do not want to be assessed. In Scotland a carer is entitled to an assessment of their needs which will be taken into account in deciding the services the person being cared for is offered.

FOR MORE INFORMATION about local authority assessment for community care services, contact the Age Concern Information Line on 0800 00 99 66. In Scotland, call the Scottish Helpline for Older People on 0845 125 9732.

PAYING FOR CARE AT HOME

This section looks at the help you can receive either from local authorities through direct payments or from the Independent Living Fund in paying for care to help you remain at home. It then explains the rules that a local authority uses when working out how much to charge you for care it has provided or arranged for you.

Direct payments

Local authorities can give people cash payments as an alternative to directly arranging community care services. Local authorities have to offer direct payments to older people who meet the eligibility requirements.

You can choose to employ a carer yourself, or use a local home care agency if you do not wish to take on the responsibility of being an employer. You may find that there is a support group in your area to help people with managing direct payments. Carers in England and Wales are also able to receive direct payments instead of services which can be provided for them.

To get a direct payment you have to be able to manage the payments, alone or with assistance. (In Scotland people who manage your affairs, such as an attorney or guardian, can have a direct payment.) They cannot usually be used to pay a spouse or close relative in the same household unless the local authority thinks this is the most appropriate way of meeting your needs. The local authority has to monitor that the money is being spent on the care you need. If you want a direct payment but your local authority refuses, you can use the complaints procedure.

FOR MORE INFORMATION about direct payments in your area, contact your local authority or the Age Concern Information Line on 0800 00 99 66. In Scotland, call the Scottish Personal Assistant Employers Network (SPAEN) on 01698 250280 or the Scottish Helpline for Older People on 0845 125 9732.

137

Individual budgets

The Government is developing and piloting 'individual budgets' as part of its 'personalisation' agenda. An individual budget is a sum of money allocated to an individual who is assessed as needing personal assistance services. An individual budget can cover more than personal social care (for example the costs of access to work, or housing support, or to pay for an adaptation). It can be a cash payment, or it can be a 'virtual' budget which is managed for you, but you know upfront how much money there is to spend over a year and decide with a support worker how you wish to design your care package.

The key features of an individual budget are:

- a transparent allocation of resources so that you know how much you have to spend on your support;

- the bringing together of a number of 'support streams' – which could include local authority provided social care, Independent Living Fund, Supporting People, access to work, disabled facilities grants, and integrated community equipment services;

- a streamlined assessment process across all agencies, meaning less time spent on giving information;

- the opportunity to use the budget in a way that best suits you;

- you can have the support of brokers, advocates or user-led organisations to help you develop your support plan and manage it; and

- the funding can be paid to you in a number of ways, depending on the amount of support you need to arrange your care.

At present individual budgets are not intended to be used for long-term residential care but this may be included in the future.

Pilot sites are being evaluated to compare the experiences of people with individual budgets to those without them, and to see how the various means tests for the different funding streams can be brought together for the purpose of creating one individual budget. The guidance on charges will be changed to reflect the new system of individual budgets.

FOR MORE INFORMATION about individual budgets, look at the In-Control website (at www.in-control.org.uk/), the Commission for Social Care Improvement's individual budget pilot programme (at http://individualbudgets.csip.org. uk/index.jsp), the Department of Health website (at www.dh.gov.uk/en /SocialCare/Socialcarereform/personalisation/individ ualbudgets/index.htm) or the National Centre for Independent Living website (at http://www.ncil.org. uk/).

Personal budgets

Personal budgets are being rolled out from April 2008 as part of the programme of transforming social care. They are intended to enable people to have much more control and the support that best suits their specific needs (this is called 'self-directed support'). They will be an upfront allocation of social care funding that individuals can use innovatively. This funding can be taken in the form of direct payments or you can continue to have the local authority pay directly for the care you want, or a combination of both.

The Independent Living Fund (ILF)

The Independent Living Fund (2006) provides cash payments to enable severely disabled people to pay for personal care or help with household tasks in order to remain living at home.

You can be considered for help from the discretionary Independent Living Fund (2006) if you are under 65 years of age when your application is received. You must also be receiving the highest care component of Disability Living Allowance, have no more than £18,500 in savings, be receiving Income Support, income-based Jobseeker's Allowance or Pension Credit guarantee credit, or not be able to afford the care you need from your income, and be receiving services or cash from the local authority, currently to the value of at least £320 a week. The maximum weekly payment from the ILF is normally £455.

FOR MORE INFORMATION about the Independent Living Fund, contact your local authority social services department, call the ILF on 0845 601 8815 or look at the website (www.ilf.org.uk).

Charges for care at home

Each local authority has discretion about whether it will charge people who receive care either provided or arranged by the local authority. Direct payments are charged for in the same way as services. Very few authorities do not charge anything.

In Scotland personal care is free if you are 65 or over, but you may still be charged for non-personal care services.

Any services arranged under Section 117 of the *Mental Health Act* for aftercare following detention in hospital must be free (however, in Scotland the different laws mean that these services may be chargeable if they are not within the definition of personal care).

Any services arranged by the NHS, such as visits by the community nurse, are also free. If you need NHS continuing healthcare in your own home, both the health element and the social care element come under the NHS and so are free (see below).

In England and Wales if your care comes under the definition of Intermediate Care (in other words, to avoid you going to hospital or when you have just come out of hospital), it will be free for six weeks. In Scotland you get free services for four weeks when you come out of hospital (even if some of the care is non-personal care).

Any charge you do pay must be 'reasonable' for you to pay, and you have the right to ask the local authority to reduce the amount or waive it altogether. It is important that the local authority is aware if you have extra costs because of your disability, such as having to pay for a gardener or someone to clean the house, or taxis because you cannot use public transport, so that it can take account of these costs. Any charge should only be based on your resources. If you disagree with your charge you can use the local authority's complaints procedure.

The Department of Health issued guidance for England (called *Fairer Charging Policies for Home Care and Other Non-Residential Social Services*) setting out a framework which local authorities must use when they decide their policies. The Welsh Assembly also produced guidance under the same name, which it revised in March 2007. The guidance is to guarantee that individuals are left with at least basic levels of income after they have been charged for the services. In England this guidance is being reviewed.

You should be left with at least £155.06 (for a single person aged 60 or over – the figures vary according to your age), and you should only be charged the full cost of the service if your capital (excluding your home) is above £22,250 in England or £22,000 in Wales. Some local authorities have set more generous capital limits and/or have set a maximum charge. Any earnings are not taken into account. The local authority should also offer to check that you are getting all the benefits you are entitled to.

In Scotland, the Convention of Scottish Local Authorities (CoSLA) has produced guidance on charging older people for 'non-personal' care services.

FOR MORE INFORMATION about charges for care at home, contact the Age Concern Information Line on 0800 00 99 66. In Scotland, call the Scottish Helpline for Older People on 0845 125 9732.

Supporting People Certain support services related to housing needs – such as community alarms and wardens – can be funded through the Supporting People fund. Supporting People is administered by the local authority and payment is made to the housing provider. Charging policies for these services must be in line with the framework of the *Fairer Charging* guidance (see above), which is used for non-residential services provided by local authorities.

FOR MORE INFORMATION, see the Age Concern Information Guide Supporting People: Paying for Supported Accommodation, *which is available from the Age Concern Information Line on 0800 00 99 66.*

Short breaks and respite care

If the local authority arranges short periods in a care home, it can charge in one of two ways as long as the stay is less than eight weeks. It can either choose to have a 'set' charge which must be reasonable, or it can use the means test used to calculate the charge for care homes (see below). The value of your home will be ignored as it counts as a temporary stay. If your care break is in hospital, arranged by the NHS, or is part of Intermediate Care, it will be free. Benefits such as Attendance Allowance may be affected, depending on how frequent your care is and how long it lasts.

PAYING FOR CARE IN A CARE HOME

This section summarises the help you can get with care home charges. The term 'care home' covers all homes that are registered homes under the *Care Standards Act 2000.* This includes independent homes and those owned by the local authority and which provide personal and/or nursing care. Before the local authority can offer any financial help you must have an assessment of your needs, as described on pages 135–136.

Please note that the information in this section does not apply to people who receive their care free under Section 117 of the Mental Health Act *(the rules are different in Scotland).*

143

In England and Wales the NHS is responsible for the funding of care provided by a registered nurse in a care home providing nursing. In England, in October 2007 the three-band system for the amount of NHS-funded nursing care was replaced by a single-band system. The single weekly rate is £101 (although this figure may be increased during the financial year).

Residents who were previously on the two rates that were lower than this were moved up to £101 on 1 October 2007. Residents who were already on the highest rate of £139 were allowed to remain on it. The only way that the £139 rate can now be lowered to £101 is if a review by the Primary Care Trust concludes that a resident's needs have reduced to a level equivalent to one of the two previous lower levels. If the person's condition is found to have deteriorated at a subsequent review, consideration should be given as to whether fully funded NHS continuing healthcare is required (see below).

In Wales there is now local discretion as to what rate is paid. Contact Age Concern Cymru at the address on page 222 for details of the rate that applies in your area.

In Scotland local authorities meet £67 towards the cost of nursing care. However, for people aged 65 and over in Scotland your personal care costs are also met (set at £149 per week).

At the same time that the new registered nursing care rules were implemented, a new framework and decision support tool was introduced for the assessment of fully funded NHS continuing healthcare. This is where, due to the resident's needs, the full cost of care, including accommodation costs, are paid for by the NHS. As well as the main tool there is a fast-track tool and a checklist.

The fast-track tool is designed to allow an urgent response where, for example, a person has a rapidly deteriorating condition. The checklist is to be used by health and social care professionals to assist in the initial decision as to whether a person's needs make them appropriate for a full NHS continuing healthcare assessment. You may want to check whether your eligibility for fully funded NHS continuing healthcare has been properly assessed.

FOR MORE INFORMATION about registered nursing care funding and NHS continuing healthcare, contact the Age Concern Information Line on 0800 00 99 66, the Scottish Helpline for Older People on 0845 125 9732 or Age Concern Cymru at the address on page 222.

If you need help with your care home costs, you can get help from the local authority and you may also get benefits from the DWP. In some circumstances Attendance Allowance or Disability Living Allowance (DLA) can be paid, as explained later.

You should be aware that although there is an assessment process and national charging procedures for care in care homes, sometimes things do not run as smoothly as described here. For example, there may be delays in obtaining an assessment, or the local authority may not agree to take financial responsibility. If you have problems, a local advice agency may be able to help.

Care arranged by the local authority

If the local authority agrees to arrange a place for you in a private or voluntary care home, it will be responsible for paying the full fee to the home and assessing your income and savings to work out how much you must pay towards the fees. If you are in a local authority home, the local authority uses the same rules to work out how much you should pay towards the cost of providing the home. You should be able to choose which home you enter, subject to certain conditions.

If the home you choose is more expensive than the local authority thinks you need, then the local authority may arrange this but you will need to make arrangements for the difference in funding to be paid. The local authority or care home provider is not allowed to make up the difference from your Personal Expenses Allowance. You normally have to make arrangements for a friend or relative to pay the difference on your behalf. In some circumstances (such as when you will eventually be selling your property) you are able to pay the top-up yourself.

If there is no suitable place at the price the local authority would usually pay for someone with your assessed needs, it will be responsible for paying for a more expensive place to meet your needs. Seek help if you cannot find a home that is suitable at the local authority price and you are being expected to pay a top-up.

Charging procedures For the local authority assessment, if you have savings of more than an upper capital limit, you will have to pay the full fee until your savings reach that amount. In England the upper capital limit is £22,250, in Wales it is £22,000 and in Scotland it is £21,500. In Scotland if you are 65 or over, your full fee is the accommodation and living costs only, as the local authority meets the personal care (£149 per week) and nursing costs (£67) of the home. If you are under 65, it just meets the nursing costs.

If you are already in a home and are using up your savings, you should apply to the local authority for help

146

a few months before your savings get down to the capital limit. (See pages 148–149 for how your former home is treated.)

For the local authority assessment, savings of no more than a lower capital limit do not have any income from them taken into account. Savings between the upper and lower capital limits will be counted as though you have an additional £1 a week income from every £250 (or part of £250). This is called 'tariff income'. In England the lower capital limit is £13,500, in Wales it is £19,000 and in Scotland £13,000.

In carrying out the assessment the local authority will take into account your income, including any Pension Credit which you are entitled to. Pension Credit is also assessed on your income and savings but the rules are different in some respects. For Pension Credit the first £10,000 of savings are ignored and every £500 (or part of £500) over £10,000 will be assumed to produce an income of £1 a week. If you are aged 60 or over, you may be able to claim Pension Credit guarantee credit whilst you are in the care home. You may also qualify for Pension Credit savings credit if you are aged 65 or over (see pages 67–72). Your appropriate amount will be calculated in the same way as if you were living in ordinary accommodation.

The local authority calculates how much you should contribute towards the cost of your care by looking at your capital and income (including tariff income). The amount which you are asked to contribute should leave you with a Personal Expenses Allowance of at least £21.15 a week in England and Scotland. In Wales it is £21.38. If you have enough qualifying income to receive Pension Credit savings credit, or do not receive this benefit because your qualifying income is too high, you should also be allowed to retain up to £5.45 (£8.15 for couples) per week of that income in addition to the Personal Expenses Allowance.

FOR MORE INFORMATION about local authority charging procedures for care homes, contact the Age Concern Information Line on 0800 00 99 66. In Scotland, call the Scottish Helpline for Older People on 0845 125 9732.

Owning your home

Local authority assessment If you are in a care home and you own your own home, its value will normally be taken into account, unless your stay is only temporary; or if your partner, a child under 16 for whom you are responsible, or a 'relative' who is either disabled or aged 60 or over, lives in the property. In addition, the value of your former home (but not of your other capital) is ignored for 12 weeks from the time you become a permanent resident. This is on top of any disregard while your stay was considered temporary. The local authority can also choose to ignore the value of your home if someone else lives there – for example, a friend aged over 60, or a relative or friend under 60 who has been caring for you for a substantial period. If the local authority says it will not use this discretion, you might want to complain through the formal complaints procedure.

If the local authority does not ignore the value of your former home (after the initial 12-week disregard), you may be able to enter into a 'deferred payment agreement' with the local authority. The local authority assists you with your fees on a loan basis but places a legal charge on the value of your property so that it can reclaim money owed to it when the property is sold. Seek legal advice before entering into a deferred payment agreement.

FOR MORE INFORMATION about who counts as a relative in this situation and about the treatment of the former home, contact the Age Concern Information Line on 0800 00 99 66. In Scotland, call the Scottish Helpline for Older People on 0845 125 9732.

The local authority is also able to take account of certain assets which you might have transferred to someone else in order to pay less for your care. It may be able to recover any debt from the recipients of such assets if the transfer was made within six months of the local authority arranging the funding of the place in the home. Even if the transfer was made more than six months before, the asset can still be taken into account.

FOR MORE INFORMATION about transfer of assets and paying for care in a care home, contact the Age Concern Information Line on 0800 00 99 66. In Scotland, call the Scottish Helpline for Older People on 0845 125 9732.

Pension Credit assessment If you move into a care home and are on Pension Credit, let The Pension Service know, as it might make a difference to the amount you receive. If you own your own home, its value will normally be taken into account when your savings are assessed for Pension Credit. However, this value will be ignored for 26 weeks, or longer if reasonable, if you are taking steps to sell it.

The value of your home will also be ignored if your spouse or partner lives there, or if a 'relative' who is either disabled or aged 60 or over lives in the property.

For more information about the system for people in care homes needing local authority support, contact the Age Concern Information Line on 0800 00 99 66. In Scotland, call the Scottish Helpline for Older People on 0845 125 9732.

Couples

When one of a couple enters a care home, the local authority will assess the amount that the resident has to pay towards the fees solely on the resident's income and savings. At the time of writing, it is expected that rules about spouses being asked to contribute to the care costs in a care home will be repealed during this year. They have already been repealed in Scotland. Local authorities have been asked to exercise their discretion not to pursue payments from spouses. An unmarried partner or civil partner has no liability under the local authority charging procedures to pay for a partner's care.

If you have an occupational or personal pension and your spouse is not also living in a care home with you, the local authority will ignore half the pension when assessing your income if you pass at least this amount to your spouse. This rule also applies to civil partners.

The local authority can also use its discretion to vary the amount of the Personal Expenses Allowance. For example, you might want to ask for this to be done if you are not married to your partner, as the local authority will not automatically ignore half of your pension in this situation.

The person at home may be able to claim benefits such as Pension Credit in their own right, depending on their income and savings.

FOR MORE INFORMATION about paying for care in a care home if you have a partner, contact the Age Concern Information Line on 0800 00 99 66. In Scotland, call the Scottish Helpline for Older People on 0845 125 9732.

Attendance Allowance or Disability Living Allowance in a care home

The mobility component of Disability Living Allowance (DLA) is not affected by admission to a care home unless you receive full funding from the NHS.

Whether or not you can receive Attendance Allowance or the care component of DLA will depend on how the fees are being met.

If you are paying the full charges in a care home or independent hospital, you can claim and receive Attendance Allowance or DLA provided you fulfil the other conditions (see pages 106–108 and 109–112). You can receive these allowances whether you arranged the admission yourself or the local authority arranged the admission. Payments for nursing care in a home providing nursing do not affect your ability to receive Attendance Allowance or DLA. In Scotland, if the local authority pays for your personal care costs, you cannot receive Attendance Allowance. If the NHS pays the full fees your Attendance Allowance or DLA will be affected as you will be regarded as a hospital inpatient (see page 114).

If you need local authority financial support in order to meet the home's fees, you cannot start to receive

Attendance Allowance or the care component of DLA. If you are already receiving one of these allowances, it will stop four weeks after the admission or sooner if you have moved in from hospital.

However, you may still retain an 'underlying entitlement' to the allowance, so that if, for example, you move out of the home, you could start receiving the allowance again without making a fresh claim. You should contact the DWP and ask for the allowance to be paid again. If the local authority temporarily provides funding but will later be reimbursed in full by you, for example under a deferred payment agreement, Attendance Allowance or the care component of DLA can be paid for that period. Pension Credit can be paid at the same time as Attendance Allowance or the care component of DLA in these circumstances, although it may not be available if you own a house which is not being marketed. Get advice if your Attendance Allowance or DLA has been stopped and you do not think that it should have been.

FOR MORE INFORMATION, see the Age Concern Information Guide Care Home Funding and Attendance Allowance, *which is available from the Age Concern Information Line on 0800 00 99 66. In Scotland, call the Scottish Helpline for Older People on 0845 125 9732.*

Other Benefits and Financial Support

This part of *Your Rights* gives details about other benefits and financial help that may be available for older people. It covers Working Tax Credit and benefits for people who are unemployed or bereaved. It then describes other types of financial support and concessions, including help with paying for fuel and other household bills, health costs and travel concessions. There is also information about help with the Council Tax.

WORKING TAX CREDIT

Working Tax Credit can be claimed by single people or couples who are employed or self-employed. There is no upper age limit for making a claim. To qualify for Working Tax Credit you must normally be living in the UK and:

- if you qualify for the 'disability element' or the '50 plus element', you must work for at least 16 hours a week; or

- if you do not qualify for these elements, you must work for at least 30 hours a week.

To qualify for the 50 plus element you must be aged 50 or over and returning to work for at least 16 hours a week after coming off certain benefits. For the six months before you started work you should have been receiving at least one of the following benefits:

- State Pension *together with either* Pension Credit;

- Jobseeker's Allowance;

- Incapacity Benefit;

- Income Support;

- Carer's Allowance;

- Bereavement Allowance; or

- Widowed Mother's Allowance.

The 50 plus element is only paid for 12 months.

You may qualify for the disability element if you have a disability which puts you at a disadvantage in getting a job and if you are, or have recently been, receiving an incapacity or disability benefit (including Incapacity

Benefit, Disability Living Allowance or Attendance Allowance).

If you fulfil these criteria, whether you will receive Working Tax Credit, and if so how much, will depend on your circumstances and your income (including that of your partner if you have one).

Working Tax Credit is administered by HM Revenue & Customs and the assessment of income and savings is done on a yearly basis. For the tax year 2008/09 any Working Tax Credit you receive will be an estimated amount based either on your previous year's income or an estimate of your current income. Your award will only be finalised after April 2009 when your actual income for 2008/09 is known. If you have been underpaid tax credits you will get the extra amount you are owed, but if you have been overpaid some tax credits you may have to pay them back, usually by recovery from next year's award.

FOR MORE INFORMATION or a claim form, contact your local Jobcentre Plus office or Tax Enquiry Centre or ring the Tax Credits Helpline on 0845 300 3900.

JOBSEEKER'S ALLOWANCE

Jobseeker's Allowance (JSA) is a taxable benefit for people who are unemployed. There are two elements: contribution-based JSA, which is based on your NI contribution record; and income-based JSA, which is means tested.

To qualify for JSA you must be:

- under State Pension age (although if you are aged 60–64 you may be better off claiming Pension Credit instead of income-based JSA);

- unemployed or working for less than 16 hours a week;

- capable of and available for work; and

- actively seeking work. You must have entered into a Jobseeker's Agreement, and you must comply with any directions given.

Contribution-based JSA can be paid for a maximum of 182 days (26 weeks) if you have paid enough National Insurance contributions. The rate for people aged 25 or over is £60.50. There are no additions for dependants. If you have an occupational or personal pension of over £50 a week, this will reduce your contribution-based JSA by the amount by which your pension exceeds £50, although in general other income you may have and your savings are not taken into account.

Income-based JSA can be paid in addition to the contribution-based JSA or on its own if you do not have sufficient NI contributions or you have already received contribution-based JSA for 26 weeks. To qualify for income-based JSA you must have no more than £16,000 savings and a low income.

If you have a partner, their income and savings will be added to yours and your partner must either not be in work or be working for less than 24 hours a week on average. Couples may be required to make a joint claim where both partners need to be actively seeking work and have entered into a Jobseeker's Agreement. If your partner is over 60 or cannot work, for example because they are disabled or are a carer, or if they are working at least 16 hours a week but less than 24, they will not have to meet the jobseeking requirements. However, if you or your partner are over 60, incapable of work because of disability or being a carer, you should consider claiming Pension Credit instead.

The amount of income-based JSA you receive will vary according to your age, your other income and savings, and entitlement to any premiums. Premiums are paid to people receiving certain disability benefits, to carers and to people with dependent children, for example.

Homeowners may get some help with certain housing costs (such as mortgage interest). When working out your benefit most of your income is taken into account, but some income, such as Disability Living Allowance, is ignored. Any capital you have above £6,000 will be assumed to produce a weekly income which will also be taken into account when calculating the amount of your benefit.

If you qualify for income-based JSA, you may also get other benefits such as Housing Benefit and Council Tax Benefit and help with NHS costs. If you are under State Pension age and do not have to attend the Jobcentre Plus office in order to receive benefit (for example because you are a carer receiving Carer's Allowance), then you can claim Income Support instead of income-based JSA. If you are aged 60 or over, you can claim Pension Credit.

How to claim

As soon as you need to look for work or need to claim benefit, you should phone Jobcentre Plus. In some areas, they will collect information over the phone and produce a statement of your circumstances for you to sign. This will mean that you might not have to complete certain claim forms. During the phone call they will ask you about your situation, and what kind of help you want. As well as offering help finding a job, they will arrange a meeting for you with a personal adviser, usually in a Jobcentre Plus office.

At the meeting, your adviser should discuss benefits and other support, as well as covering employment options. At the end of the interview you will have to sign a Jobseeker's Agreement which outlines the action you are expected to take to find work. Once JSA is awarded, you will need to attend your local office, usually every two weeks.

In some situations benefit may be stopped for a limited period. For example, if you leave work voluntarily without 'just cause' or refuse a job without 'good cause', then you may lose benefit for up to 26 weeks. You may lose benefit if you accept early retirement, although not if you are made redundant.

> FOR MORE INFORMATION *if you are refused benefit or need help or advice with claiming JSA, contact a local advice agency.*

Schemes to help people back to work

The Government's 'New Deal' programme aims to help people into work. It includes the New Deal for Disabled People and the New Deal 25 plus for long-term unemployed people. There is also a New Deal 50 plus for people aged over 50.

Under the New Deal 50 plus programme people are offered assistance from a personal adviser, job search support, access to other Jobcentre Plus programmes, and an in-work training grant. You may also get financial help from the 50 plus element of Working Tax Credit.

There are also other specific measures to encourage people to work, including the continuation of Housing Benefit and Council Tax Benefit for an extra four weeks after you start work and your JSA stops.

FOR MORE INFORMATION, contact your local Jobcentre Plus office.

INCOME SUPPORT

Income Support is a benefit which is based on income and savings, and which is intended to help with basic weekly living costs. The information here applies to people under 60 – when you reach 60 you may be able to get Pension Credit instead (see pages 50–75). Income Support is paid to people who do not have to sign on for work; for example, people who can't work because they are carers or people who are sick or disabled.

Income Support can be paid on its own if you have no other income, or it can top up other benefits or part-time earnings. If you don't have much money coming in and have no more than £16,000 in savings, it is worth checking to see if you can qualify for Income Support. If you have a partner, their income and savings will be added to yours. You cannot get Income Support if you work 16 hours a week or more or if your partner works 24 hours a week or more.

The amount of Income Support you receive will vary according to your age, your other income and savings, and entitlement to any premiums. Premiums are paid to people receiving certain disability benefits, to carers and to people with dependent children, for example. Homeowners may get some help with certain housing costs (such as mortgage interest). When working out your benefit most of your income is taken into account, but some income, such as Disability Living Allowance, is ignored. Any capital you have above £6,000 will be assumed to produce a weekly income which will also be taken into account when calculating the amount of your benefit.

To claim income support, contact your local Jobcentre Plus office. If you need more advice about Income Support, contact a local advice agency.

BEREAVEMENT BENEFITS

Bereavement Benefits are generally available to men and women under State Pension age when their husband, wife or civil partner dies. Entitlement is based on the National Insurance contribution record of the person who has died. Information given here covers the Bereavement Payment and the Bereavement Allowance. There is also a Widowed Parent's Allowance for people with dependent children. For more information on this, contact a local advice agency or Jobcentre Plus office.

When you register a death the Registrar will give you Form BD8 (Form 344S1 in Scotland) to send to your local Jobcentre Plus or pension centre. If you wish to claim Bereavement Benefits, answer 'yes' to the appropriate question on the reverse of the form.

People over State Pension age whose husband, wife or civil partner dies may be entitled to claim a State Pension based on their late partner's contributions, as explained on pages 9–11.

Women widowed before 9 April 2001 may be receiving Widow's Pension (see page 162).

Any earnings you receive will not affect your Bereavement Benefits, Widow's Pension or State Pension.

Bereavement Payment

The Bereavement Payment is a single lump-sum payment of £2,000. It is tax free and is paid mainly to people under State Pension age. If you are over State Pension age when your husband, wife or civil partner dies, you can qualify for a payment if:

- your partner was under State Pension age when they died; or

- your partner was over State Pension age when they died but not entitled to a State Pension based on their own contribution record (for example, if your wife was over State Pension age when she died and she only received the 'married woman's pension' based on your contributions).

Bereavement Allowance

The Bereavement Allowance is paid to both men and women who are aged at least 45 but under State Pension age when they are bereaved and whose husband, wife or civil partner fulfilled the contribution conditions. The full standard rate of £90.70 is paid if you are aged 55 or over when you are bereaved. If you are aged 45 to 54, you will receive a percentage of the standard rate. You cannot receive any of your partner's Additional State Pension.

Bereavement Allowance will be paid for a maximum of 52 weeks but will stop if you remarry, form a civil partnership, live with someone as though you were married or civil partners, or reach State Pension age during that period. Once you reach State Pension age you may be able to claim a State Pension based on your late husband, wife or civil partner's contributions, as explained on pages 9–11.

Widow's Pension

If your husband died before 9 April 2001, you may be in receipt of a Widow's Pension and this will not have been affected by the introduction of Bereavement Benefits. The full standard rate is £90.70 but you may be getting less if you were under 55 when you were widowed.

You may also be receiving an Additional State Pension based on your husband's earnings since 1978, taking into account any periods that he was contracted out of SERPS.

When you reach State Pension age (currently 60 for women born on or before 5 April 1950), you can draw the State Pension instead of the Widow's Pension or you can remain on the Widow's Pension until you reach 65. The amounts will often be the same, but you may also receive some Graduated Pension with the State Pension. Check with the DWP what the different amounts would be.

The Widow's Pension will not be affected by your earnings. However, if you do not draw your State Pension at the age of 60, you will not earn extra pension unless you give up the Widow's Pension. If you remarry or form a civil partnership before you reach 60, you will lose the Widow's Pension. It will also be suspended during any period when you live with someone as their partner. However, if you are 60 or over and receive a State Pension based on your previous husband's contributions, you will not lose this if you remarry or live with someone as though you were married or civil partners.

FOR MORE INFORMATION, see DWP guide NP45 A Guide to Bereavement Benefits, *which is only available on the website (www.dwp.gov.uk), and Jobcentre Plus leaflet WIDA5* If You Are Widowed or Your Civil Partner Dies.

HOUSEHOLD BILLS, INSULATION AND REPAIRS

This section looks at some of the main household bills and expenses that older people face. It briefly covers dealing with debt and then summarises the help that may be available for different expenses, referring you to Age Concern information sheets and other sources where appropriate. More detailed information is given about: paying for fuel and insulation; help with repairs; and the Council Tax.

Debt problems

Many older people have to manage on low incomes and sometimes face particular problems when an unexpected bill comes in or income drops because of a change in circumstances, such as divorce or bereavement. If you are having difficulty managing, check to see whether you are entitled to any additional income such as the benefits described in this book (for example Pension Credit, Housing Benefit or Council Tax Benefit). Then write down the amount of money you need for essential everyday living. This should help you to work out a statement of income and expenditure which you can then use to negotiate smaller payments to your creditors. Many people underestimate their basic living expenses and then try to pay their bills at a higher rate than they can really afford. Once they see the reality of your situation, most creditors should freeze interest and accept payments that you can afford.

If this seems too much to have to deal with, seek advice. There are many independent advice agencies which can help with debt problems, including Citizens Advice, or you can ring National Debtline on Freephone 0808 808 4000.

FOR MORE INFORMATION, see the Age Concern Information Guide Dealing with Debt, *which is available from the Age Concern Information Line on 0800 00 99 66.*

Help with bills and expenses

Fuel: There are no regular weekly social security payments towards fuel bills but there are Winter Fuel Payments and Cold Weather Payments, as described below. Grants towards insulation and draught proofing may help you heat your home more effectively. Some fuel companies have charitable trusts to help vulnerable customers with fuel debts. Help is discretionary and criteria for eligibility are set by individual companies.

Rent and mortgage costs: Means-tested help towards rent comes through Housing Benefit (see pages 76–99), while homeowners may get help with their mortgage interest payments and certain service charges through Pension Credit (see pages 50–75) or Income Support or income-based JSA if aged under 60 (see pages 155–160).

Council Tax: Council Tax Benefit (see pages 76–99) is means tested. There are also other ways of reducing Council Tax bills, which are described on pages 176–178.

Water charges: There are no social security benefits to help with the cost of water or sewerage charges. Some water companies have charitable trusts to help vulnerable customers with water debts. Help is discretionary and criteria for eligibility are set by individual companies. Some customers may be able to get help with the costs of water supply under the Vulnerable Groups Scheme (WaterSure). This scheme is open to people who are receiving certain qualifying benefits and who have water meters and use a high volume of water because of certain medical conditions, or because they have three or more children under the age of 19 and in full-time education living in the property. Contact your water company for more information.

The system is different in Scotland. There is only one supplier of water and sewerage services in Scotland – Scottish Water.

FOR MORE INFORMATION on services, contact Scottish Water on 0845 601 8855 (for emergencies 0845 600 8855) or contact the Scottish Helpline for Older People on 0845 125 9732.

Telephone costs: There is no national scheme providing financial help with phone charges. Some people who are ill or disabled may be able to receive help from their local authority social services department. This help could include a payment to cover the installation costs of the phone and sometimes the rental costs. The local authority may also help with aids and adaptations to the phone; for example, lamp signalling handsets for people with hearing difficulties. If you have been on Pension Credit, Income Support or income-based Jobseeker's Allowance for at least 26 weeks, you may be able to get a loan from the Social Fund (see pages 99–104) to cover the cost of installing a phone.

Repairs, improvements and adaptations: In some situations you may be able to receive a grant to help with household repairs, adaptations or improvements, as explained on pages 173–176.

PAYING FOR FUEL AND INSULATION

The cost of fuel is a major expense for most pensioners. This section outlines what help is available.

Fuel debts

If you have a fuel debt and are receiving Pension Credit, Income Support or income-based Jobseeker's Allowance (JSA), you may be able to avoid disconnection or get reconnected by going on 'fuel direct'. Some of your benefit will be withheld every week and paid direct to the company. If you think that too large an amount is being withheld, ask the DWP whether the company will accept a smaller amount.

All gas and electricity suppliers must offer special services to people of pensionable age and people who have a disability or a long-term illness. These services include:

- if you are on means-tested benefits, you can ask for a free gas safety check each year (you have to own your home and all adults in the household have to be eligible for free services);

- a quarterly meter reading on request if no one in the house can read the meter; and

- you can ask for bills to be sent to a nominated third party for payment.

There is also a code of practice which requires suppliers not to disconnect supplies to households where all the occupants are pensioners for non-payment of bills (provided this is not deliberate) during the winter months.

Winter Fuel Payments

Winter Fuel Payments provide help with the cost of fuel bills for pensioner households. They are paid to most people aged 60 or over living in the UK, there are no income or savings limits, and they are not taxable. The payments for each year are based on someone's age during the qualifying week during that year, which is normally the week beginning with the third Monday in September.

The Winter Fuel Payment is normally £200 for most households with someone aged 60 or over during the qualifying week. Since Winter 2003/04, an extra £100 is paid where someone in the household is aged 80 or over.

For Winter 2008/09, the Chancellor announced in the March 2008 Budget an additional one-off payment of £50 for households with someone aged 60 or over and £100 where there is someone aged 80 or over. This will be paid with the Winter Fuel Payments. Although full details are not available at the time of writing, it is expected to follow the rules as set out below.

If you or your partner do not receive Pension Credit or income-based Jobseeker's Allowance – for Winter 2008/09:

- If you are aged 60 to 79, you should get £250 if you are the only person in the household entitled to a payment, or £125 if you share a household with one or more other people entitled to a payment – for example, a married couple, or two friends living together, will each receive £125.

- If you are aged 80 or over, you will get £400 if you are the only person in the household aged 80 or over, or £200 each if there are more people aged 80 or over entitled to a payment.

If you are receiving Pension Credit or income-based Jobseeker's Allowance – for Winter 2008/09:

- If you are single, you should get £250 (£400 if you are 80 or over), regardless of who else is in the household.

- If you are one of a couple and the Pension Credit or income-based Jobseeker's Allowance is in your name, then you will receive £250 (or £400 if you or your partner is aged 80 or over) – if your partner made the claim, they will receive the payment.

Some people are not eligible for payments – for example people who have been living in a care home for 13 weeks or more by the qualifying week who receive Pension Credit or income-based JSA, and people who have been in hospital for more than 52 weeks, will not get a payment. People living in a care home who are not excluded because of the benefits they receive will normally get £100 (£150 if they are 80 or over). At the time of writing, it is not known whether or not the additional one-off payment for Winter 2008/09 will apply to people in care homes.

If you are receiving a State Pension, or certain other social security benefits (excluding Housing Benefit and Council Tax Benefit), or if you received a payment last winter and your circumstances have not changed, then you should not need to claim as payments will normally be made automatically before Christmas. In other circumstances – for example if you are a man aged 60 not receiving any State benefits – you will need to make a claim.

FOR MORE INFORMATION or to make a claim, contact The Pension Service's Winter Fuel Helpline on 08459 151 515.

If you need to make a claim for the payment for Winter 2008/09, your claim must be received by 30 March 2009. However, there is no time limit for claims for the first three winters (1997/98, 1998/99 and 1999/2000).

Although payments are normally only made to people living in the UK, some people who qualify for a Winter Fuel Payment in the UK and move to another European Economic Area country or Switzerland, may be able to continue to receive payments. For more information on this specific issue ring 029 2042 8635.

Cold Weather Payments

If you receive Pension Credit, Income Support or income-based JSA, you may be eligible for Cold Weather Payments. If you are receiving Income Support or income-based JSA, this must include a pensioner or disability premium. A payment of £8.50 is made when the average temperature at a specified weather station has been recorded as, or is forecast to be, 0° Celsius or below over seven consecutive days. Savings are not taken into account. These payments will be made automatically, so you do not have to make a claim.

Grants for energy efficiency

If you live in England Warm Front is a government-funded scheme set up to provide energy advice and grants to improve home energy efficiency. It is available to certain groups of people who own or privately rent their home and who are in receipt of qualifying benefits.

The Warm Front provides a package of energy efficiency insulation and heating measures tailored to each property, up to the value of £2,700 (or up to the value of £4,000 where oil central heating is installed or repaired). It may include gas, electric or oil-fired central heating, cavity and loft insulation, draught proofing, hot water tank insulation, converting a solid-fuel open fire to a modern glass-fronted fire, energy efficiency advice and low-energy light bulbs.

Households that have already received assistance from Warm Front are able to apply for additional measures. The value of the grant available to properties previously helped will be the balance of £2,700 (or £4,000 if oil central heating is involved) less the value of all works completed since June 2000.

The Warm Front grant is available to householders who are aged 60 or over and in receipt of Pension Credit, Housing Benefit, Council Tax Benefit, Income Support or income-based Jobseeker's Allowance. It is also available to those who have young children or who are disabled and receive qualifying income-related or disability-related benefits. Householders whose spouse, civil partner or partner fulfils the eligibility criteria are also eligible. A partner means a person with whom the applicant lives as if they were husband and wife or civil partner.

The Warm Front schemes are being promoted and run by the Eaga Partnership Ltd, the managing organisation appointed by the Government. Eaga will arrange for a surveyor to visit and assess what work needs to be done. In rented accommodation, the landlord's consent is needed before any work can be undertaken. Landlords must not put rent up because of the improvements funded by the Warm Front for a set period of time (one year following insulation works or two years following heating works).

Householders who are aged 60 or over and are *not* entitled to the Warm Front Grant can receive a grant up to a maximum of £300 (the Heating Rebate) for the provision or replacement of certain heating systems. Qualifying applicants will have to use one of the installers approved by Eaga and the payment will be made directly to the installer on completion of the work.

FOR MORE INFORMATION, contact the Age Concern Information Line on 0800 00 99 66 or EAGA on 0800 316 6011.

If you live in Wales The Home Energy Efficiency Scheme in Wales (HEES Wales) provides grants for people aged 60 or over who are receiving one of the following income-related benefits: Pension Credit, Housing Benefit, Council Tax Benefit, income-based Jobseeker's Allowance or certain disability benefits, including Disability Living Allowance and Attendance Allowance. The grant may offer a variety of insulation measures, including cavity wall loft insulation, draught proofing and a range of heating improvements, including the installation of gas or electric central heating for those without central heating, the conversion of an existing solid fuel system, repairs to systems that are not working, energy efficiency advice, smoke alarms and a benefit entitlement check. If you are aged 60 or over, own your home and are not on any benefit, you may be eligible for a 25 per cent grant towards the cost of the above measures up to £500. Other householders may also qualify for the scheme as eligibility varies.

If you live in Scotland In Scotland energy efficiency grants are made under the Warm Deal scheme. The grant covers a package of energy efficiency measures, all or some of which may be offered, according to the energy needs of the home. Grants may be offered to homeowners and tenants (including council tenants) who receive any or several of the following income-related benefits: Pension Credit, Housing Benefit, Council Tax Benefit, income-based Jobseeker's Allowance or certain disability benefits, including Disability Living Allowance or Attendance Allowance.

The maximum grant is £500 and may cover: cavity wall insulation; loft insulation; draught proofing; hot and cold tank and pipe insulation; energy efficiency advice; and up to four energy-efficient light bulbs. The scheme is administered by Scottish Gas, who can arrange for a registered installer to do the work. If you want to carry out the work yourself, a lower grant of up to £40 is available to cover the cost of materials, but you must not buy any materials until authorised by Scottish Gas. Those over 60, but not in receipt of any of the benefits listed above, may qualify for a reduced grant of £125 or 25 per cent of the cost of the work, whichever is the lower.

The Scottish Government provides non-means-tested grants for the installation of central heating and insulation. If you, or your partner, are aged 60 or over, you may get central heating installed if you have no central heating or your system is 'broken and beyond repair'. If you are aged 60 or over and receive Pension Credit guarantee credit, or you are aged 80 or over, you may also qualify for an upgraded system if yours is partial or inefficient. There are no retrospective grants, so you cannot claim for heating that has already been installed.

If you own your home or rent your home from a private landlord, phone Scottish Gas (which runs the programme on behalf of the Scottish Government) on Freephone 0800 316 1653 or 6009. If you are the tenant of a local authority or housing association, and you do not have central heating, contact your landlord.

HELP WITH REPAIRS, IMPROVEMENTS AND ADAPTATIONS

England and Wales

Local authorities (councils) have general powers to provide assistance for repairs, improvements and adaptations to housing. The assistance provided by the local authority may be provided in any form, including loans, grants, labour, materials or advice. It might be provided unconditionally, or subject to conditions such as repayment of all or part of the assistance or a contribution towards the work for which assistance is required. The local authority must publish a policy setting out the type of assistance it will provide and in what circumstances. It should also tell you how to make an enquiry and apply for assistance. A summary of the policy must be available to the public on request.

Local authorities also provide disabled facilities grants, which are mandatory in specific circumstances. A grant must be given if you are disabled and do not have access to your home and to the basic amenities within it (such as a bathroom, toilet or kitchen), provided that you qualify on income grounds – the grants are means tested. If you receive Pension Credit guarantee credit, Income Support or income-based Jobseeker's Allowance you will not normally have to make a contribution.

173

FOR MORE INFORMATION, contact the local authority or other agency, such as a local Age Concern, as the system is complicated. A step-by-step guide on how to work out your contribution is included in The Disability Rights Handbook *(see page 211).*

The formal application for the grant must be made to the housing department of the local authority. The housing department must consult with the social services department to decide if the adaptations are necessary and appropriate. This will normally mean that you will receive a visit from an occupational therapist from social services to assess your needs and make recommendations on what work needs to be done.

The maximum amount for a mandatory disabled facilities grant is £25,000 in England and £30,000 in Wales.

In addition, local authorities are able to give discretionary assistance for adaptations or to help the occupant to move to alternative, more suitable accommodation. There is no restriction on the amount of assistance that may be given. It may be paid in addition, or as an alternative to, the grant. You should not start the work or buy any of the materials until you have received the local authority's approval to go ahead.

In England, minor adaptations costing less than £1,000, and equipment that helps disabled people to manage daily tasks around the home, are required to be provided free of charge to those who are eligible.

If you receive Pension Credit, Income Support or income-based Jobseeker's Allowance, you may be able to claim a discretionary Community Care Grant or Budgeting Loan for minor household repairs (see pages 99–104).

In some areas there are Home Improvement Agencies (sometimes called Care and Repair or Staying Put projects) which provide support for vulnerable people, such as older people or disabled people, who are homeowners or who live in private rented accommodation, to help them undertake repairs, improvements or adaptations to their home. Your local authority or local Age Concern should know whether there is a scheme in your area, or you can contact Foundations, the national co-ordinating body for Home Improvement Agencies, at the address on page 208.

FOR MORE INFORMATION, contact the Age Concern Information Line on 0800 00 99 66.

Scotland

In Scotland the system of grants is different and only brief information is given here. Grants may be available from the local authority housing department to owners and, in certain circumstances, private tenants to help meet the cost of improvement and repair work. The amount of grant you receive depends on your financial circumstances, but in some cases a minimum grant of 50 per cent will be available. Most grants are discretionary but you must be awarded a grant in some circumstances; for example if your home lacks certain standard amenities. You may also get help towards the costs of housing aids and adaptations if you are assessed by the social work department as needing these. In such cases the minimum 50 per cent grant applies. Some Care and Repair schemes may be able to help you through the process of applying for a grant.

FOR DETAILS OF GRANTS, or to find out about Care and Repair in your area, contact your local authority housing department or the Scottish Helpline for Older People on 0845 125 9732 or see Age Concern Scotland Factsheet 13s Older Homeowners: Financial Help with Repairs and Adaptations.

HELP WITH THE COUNCIL TAX

The Council Tax is the system of paying towards local government services in England, Scotland and Wales. The rates system continues in Northern Ireland, with a new Rate Relief Scheme for people with incomes just outside the limit for Housing Benefit or who are only getting partial help with their rates.

Under the Council Tax system all domestic dwellings are allocated to one of eight bands (A–H), depending on their estimated value in April 1991. The level of tax for a property in band H will be three times as high as the tax for a property in band A. The banding system in Wales has changed to nine bands (A–I), based on property values in April 2003.

One bill will be sent to each household. One or more people will be legally responsible for paying the bill, although the household can choose how to divide up the bill.

Reducing your bill

There are various ways that your bill may be reduced and these are summarised below. It may be possible to receive help from more than one of these schemes.

Exemptions Some properties, mainly certain empty ones, will be exempt, which means that there will be no Council Tax to pay. For example, your former home will be exempt if it is empty because you are living in a hospital or care home, or because you have gone to live with someone else in order to receive or provide personal care. A property is also exempt if a 'severely mentally impaired' person lives there alone and would be liable to pay the tax.

Disability reduction scheme The property may be placed in a lower band if it has certain features which are important for a disabled person, such as extra space for a wheelchair or an additional bathroom or kitchen for the use of the disabled person. If your home qualifies for a reduction, your bill will be reduced to the level of tax for the band below the one your home is in. Since April 2000, properties in the lowest band (A) that have the relevant disability features have also qualified for a reduction. In this situation bills will be reduced by one sixth. Contact your local authority if you think that your property would qualify for a reduction.

Discounts The Council Tax rules assume that there are two or more people living in each property. A discount of a quarter (25 per cent) will be given if someone lives alone and a discount of half (50 per cent) will normally be given if no one is living there. Some people will not be counted for the purposes of the Council Tax, so discounts may still be given even if there are two or more people in a property. For example, someone who is 'severely mentally impaired' will not be counted. The discount can also apply to a carer who lives with and, for at least 35 hours a week, is caring for someone receiving the highest care component of Disability Living Allowance or the higher rate of Attendance Allowance. You will not be able to get this discount if the person you care for is your partner or is a child under 18.

Council Tax Benefit This depends on the income and savings of the person(s) responsible for the bill or the people they live with. It is described in more detail on pages 76–99.

FOR MORE INFORMATION, contact the Age Concern Information Line on 0800 00 99 66.

HELP WITH HEALTH COSTS

Most of the treatment given under the National Health Service (NHS) is free, but there are some things for which most people have to pay part or all of the cost. This section first outlines hearing and chiropody services. It then explains who can get help with the cost of other NHS services such as dental care, eye tests and glasses.

Free NHS services

Hearing aids You should discuss hearing difficulties with your GP who may, if necessary, refer you to a hospital for tests. If you are prescribed a hearing aid, this will be fitted and issued by a local NHS hearing aid centre. NHS hearing aids are available on free loan; repairs and batteries are also free. It is possible to buy private hearing aids, but these can be expensive and are not necessarily more effective.

FOR MORE INFORMATION, contact the Royal National Institute for Deaf People (address on page 209), which publishes a range of information leaflets on hearing loss, hearing aids (including digital hearing aids) and other matters concerning deafness.

Chiropody/podiatry NHS chiropody/podiatry services are free to those with a clinical need. In many areas, there are eligibility criteria which you must meet in order to be treated as an NHS patient. Your GP or Primary Care Trust should be able to advise you about local NHS chiropody/podiatry services.

Some chiropody services are liaising with voluntary organisations, such as Age Concern, to provide nail cutting services and education in foot care to prevent problems. The Age Concern Information Line on Freephone 0800 00 99 66 can give you the contact details for your nearest Age Concern. Contact Age Concern locally to see if it offers this service and whether there is a charge.

If you wish to consider private treatment, your local NHS chiropody department may have details of private practitioners. Alternatively, you may wish to refer to *Yellow Pages* or look at the website of the Society of Chiropodists and Podiatrists (www.feetforlife.org). Make sure that the chiropodist is registered with the Health Professions Council.

Help with NHS costs

If you (or your partner if you have one) receive Pension Credit guarantee credit, Income Support or income-based Jobseeker's Allowance (JSA), you are entitled to receive full help with the health costs described below by showing your award letter from the DWP. If you receive Working Tax Credit with Child Tax Credit or with a disability element (check your award letter), you may also get this help, depending on the level of your income. In the following paragraphs, wherever Pension Credit guarantee credit or Income Support are mentioned it also covers these other benefits. In certain circumstances help may also be available to people receiving a War Pension.

179

If you are not in receipt of one of the benefits mentioned above but are on a low income and have no more than £16,000 in savings, you can apply for help with costs of NHS dental treatment, glasses or contact lenses, and hospital travel costs through the NHS Low Income Scheme. (The limit for people living permanently in care homes is different – £21,500.)

If you qualify for help with health costs, you will be sent one of two certificates. Certificate HC2 entitles you to full help with health costs, including free prescriptions, dental treatment, glasses or hospital travel costs. If your income is higher, you may get certificate HC3, which entitles you to partial help with health costs. The HC3 does not entitle you to any help with prescription charges if you would normally pay. If you are single and over 65, or one of a couple where at least one of you is over 65, and your only income is State benefit related, your HC2 or HC3 certificate will usually be awarded for five years; otherwise a certificate will be awarded for one year.

To apply for a certificate you will need to complete the form HC1. This is available from the DWP or your local NHS hospital; some dentists, opticians and GP surgeries also have them. (If you live permanently in a care home and receive financial support from the local authority, ask the owner of the home for form HC1 (SC).) It is best to apply in advance. Remember that if you receive Pension Credit guarantee credit, you do not need to apply for a certificate.

FOR MORE INFORMATION, see Department of Health leaflet HC11 Help with Health Costs *or the Age Concern Information Guide* Help with Health Costs *(which is available from the Age Concern Information Line on 0800 00 99 66).*

Prescriptions NHS prescriptions are free to people aged 60 or over. However, younger adults can also get free prescriptions if they have a low income or suffer from a 'specified medical condition' (these are listed in leaflet HC11) and hold an exemption certificate.

Prescriptions are free to partners aged under 60 of people receiving Pension Credit guarantee credit and those who have a valid certificate HC2 on grounds of low income, as described above. People who have a valid certificate HC3 entitling them to partial help with some NHS costs cannot get free prescriptions.

If you cannot get free prescriptions but require regular prescriptions, in England you may be able to save money by buying a prescription pre-payment certificate (PPC) for either 4 or 12 months. To help spread the cost of a 12-month PPC, you can now choose to pay by 10 monthly direct debit instalments.

FOR MORE INFORMATION about the PPC scheme or to request an application form (FP95), you can ring 0845 850 00 30. The form is also available from pharmacists. Your pharmacist can help you decide whether a PPC would be financially advantageous for you.

In Wales, prescriptions have been free for everyone since April 2007.

Dental care NHS dental treatment, check-ups and dentures are free if you or your partner gets Pension Credit guarantee credit or if you have certificate HC2. The cost may be reduced if you have certificate HC3. Details of how to apply for a certificate are given above. Every time you start a new course of treatment, tell the dentist that you are on Pension Credit guarantee credit or

181

have certificate HC2 or HC3. In Wales, dental checks are free for all people aged 60 and over.

The NHS operates a three-band system of patient charging per course of treatment in England and Wales. Unless you are entitled to free treatment or help with the cost of treatment, in England you will pay either £16.20 (Band 1), £44.60 (Band 2) or £198.00 (Band 3), depending on which band the most expensive part of your treatment falls into. In Wales, the bands are £12 (Band 1), £39 (Band 2) or £177 (Band 3).

> *FOR INFORMATION about which local dentists are offering NHS treatment, contact NHS Direct on 0845 46 47 if you live in England or Wales, or look at the NHS Choices website (at www.nhs.uk). In Scotland, call the NHS Helpline on 0800 22 44 88 (please note this is not an emergency dental service) or call The Scottish Helpline for Older People on 0845 125 9732.*

No help is given towards private dental fees. If you want NHS dental care, make sure that the dentist is providing you with NHS treatment before you start each course of treatment. You can do this when you discuss the proposed treatment with your dentist.

Sight tests and glasses NHS funded sight tests are available to all people aged 60 or over. There is no definition of what an NHS sight test should include. Tests for conditions such as glaucoma and other eye diseases that are more likely in older people are particularly important, so always ask what tests will be included in your sight test.

Partners of people receiving Pension Credit guarantee credit who are under the age of 60 are entitled to an NHS funded sight test. It is recommended that younger adults have a sight test every two years and those aged 70 and over have one every 12 months. Younger people also qualify for an NHS funded sight test if they or their partner have certificate HC2, as described above. NHS funded sight tests are also available to people who belong to a priority group, which includes registered blind and partially sighted people, those who need complex lenses, and diagnosed diabetics. People who have glaucoma or are considered to be at risk of glaucoma, or someone aged 40 or over who is the parent, brother, sister or son or daughter of a person with diagnosed glaucoma, also qualify for NHS funded sight tests.

If, for health reasons, you cannot get to the optician's practice for a sight test, you may be able to arrange for an optician to visit you at home. If you are entitled to an NHS funded sight test, you will not have to pay for the visit.

You are entitled to a voucher towards the cost of glasses provided you or your partner get Pension Credit guarantee credit or have certificate HC2. You may get some help if you have certificate HC3. You may be able to claim a refund in some circumstances if you do not receive your certificate in time, but it is better to apply well in advance. If you require two different pairs of glasses – one for reading, one for distance – you are entitled to two vouchers.

The voucher carries a financial value linked to your optical prescription; it may cover the full cost of the glasses or be used as part-payment for a more expensive pair. If your glasses or contact lenses cost more than any voucher you are given, you will have to pay the difference. If you need complex lenses, you will be able to receive a voucher from your optician to help pay for

183

the glasses regardless of income and savings. However, the amount of help will be greater if you or your partner receives Pension Credit guarantee credit or qualifies on grounds of low income.

You do not have to get your glasses from the optician who carries out your sight test, although you may choose to do so. If you prefer to obtain your glasses from a different optician, simply take your prescription (and any voucher to which you are entitled) with you. Before you have a sight test or buy glasses, find out whether you qualify for help. If you will have to pay some or all of the cost, it is best to 'shop around' to check whether another optician might be cheaper, as charges can vary.

People with serious eye conditions and who require specialist hospital care only have to pay up to a maximum charge and the hospital then meets the difference between the maximum charge and the cost of the glasses.

FOR MORE INFORMATION on eye problems and NHS funded sight tests, contact the Royal National Institute of Blind People at the address on page 209.

Elastic hosiery, wigs, fabric supports Elastic support stockings are available on prescription, and are free to both men and women aged 60 or over. Support tights are available only through the hospital service but are free to people who are entitled to free prescriptions; for example if they receive Pension Credit guarantee credit or have certificate HC2.

Wigs and fabric supports are supplied through hospitals and are free for inpatients. If you are an outpatient, there are charges depending on the type of wig or fabric support supplied. However, they are free if you are on Pension Credit guarantee credit or have certificate HC2; if you have certificate HC3, you may get some help with the cost.

Hospital travel costs If you get Pension Credit guarantee credit, you are entitled to help with the necessary costs of travelling to and from hospital (or other place) for NHS treatment under the care of a consultant. If you have certificate HC2 or HC3 on grounds of low income, you may get help towards these costs. See 'Help with NHS costs' above on how to apply for a certificate. If you are not sure what help you can get, contact the hospital before you travel. Hospitals will not normally reimburse taxi fares unless taxis are the only transport available – check with the hospital first.

If you qualify for help with travel costs and it is medically necessary for you to have a companion to accompany you, their travel costs should also be covered. However, they can only be claimed when they are certified to be necessary in the opinion of a doctor or appropriate health professional – so check with the hospital before you travel to ensure that you have the necessary permission or written confirmation.

There is no government scheme to help with costs of travelling to hospital to visit relatives or friends in hospital. However, if you are visiting a close relative in hospital and you receive Pension Credit (guarantee and/or savings credit), you may be able to get help with the cost of your fares from the Social Fund (see pages 99–104).

Healthcare outside the UK

As a UK resident, you are covered by the NHS only while you are in the UK. If you are abroad on business

185

or on holiday and fall ill, you may have to pay all or part of the cost of any treatment. There are special arrangements with member states of the European Economic Area (EEA) plus Switzerland (see page vii), which may entitle you to free or reduced-cost state-provided emergency treatment. If you are in one of these countries, you must show your credit-card-sized plastic EHIC (European Health Insurance Card) to the doctor working for the state health system.

If you do not have an EHIC, you can apply by:

- calling the EHIC Application Line on 0845 606 2030. Your card will be delivered within 10 working days;

- completing an application form online (at www.ehic.org.uk). Your card will be delivered within 7 working days; or

- picking up an application form from a post office and returning your completed form to the address indicated. Your card will be delivered within 21 working days.

You will need to have your NHS number or National Insurance number to hand when you apply. The EHIC is valid for five years.

FOR MORE INFORMATION about an EHIC, or if you lose your EHIC, contact the EHIC enquiry line on 0845 605 0707.

The EHIC is not a substitute for holiday insurance and will only provide you with basic medical care in the event of an emergency. Not all doctors practising in an EEA country will be working within the state health system. So if you do have to visit a doctor in the community for emergency treatment, you will need to check whether your EHIC is acceptable to secure treatment and any medication necessary free of charge or at a reduced cost. You will also need to check that any hospital you visit for emergency treatment is part of the state health system.

It is advisable to take out private medical insurance to cover the full cost of any treatment you may need abroad, whether you are going to an EEA or non-EEA country.

When taking out insurance it is important that you declare pre-existing conditions you currently have or have had in the past, such as a heart attack. If you don't, you may not be covered by your policy should you make a claim. Medical treatment is very expensive, as is the cost of bringing a person back to the UK in the event of illness or death.

> *FOR MORE INFORMATION, see the booklet* Health Advice for Travellers, *which is available from post offices. It contains information about non-EEA countries that the UK has reciprocal medical care agreements with and what you may be entitled to if you are taken ill. It also gives general guidance on immunisation requirements for travellers.*

You are entitled to typhoid, polio and hepatitis A vaccines on the NHS: their administration is free and prescription charges follow the patient's normal entitlement (free for people aged 60 and over, for example). All other travel immunisations are non-NHS and are likely to incur a variable charge.

If you are going to live permanently or for a large part of the year in another country, find out well in advance about your entitlement to medical treatment there. If you plan to return to the UK for holidays or for longer periods of time, you should also check your entitlement to treatment while you are back in the UK. Legislation passed in 2004 allows those in receipt of a UK State Pension and who spend at least six months of the year living in the UK – living the remainder of the year in an EEA country – to be exempt from charges for NHS treatment they receive while in the UK. This exemption does not apply if time outside the UK is spent in a non-EEA country.

TRAVEL

Rail and underground

All rail companies give one-third reductions on most types of ticket to people who have a Senior Railcard, which currently costs £24 and is valid for one year. It is available to people aged 60 or over, provided proof of age is given.

LEAFLETS WITH APPLICATION FORMS should be available from any staffed railway stations or rail-appointed travel agents, by phone from National Rail Enquiries on 08457 48 49 50 or from the website (www.senior-railcard.co.uk).

If you are disabled, you can buy a Disabled Person's Railcard, which currently costs £18 for one year or £48 for three years, and which allows you and a companion to travel at a third off most standard fares.

APPLICATION FORMS AND FULL DETAILS OF WHO QUALIFIES are available from many railway stations or from the Disabled Persons Railcard Office at the address on page 207 or the website (www.disabledpersons-railcard.co.uk).

People travelling in their own wheelchair who do not hold the Railcard can get discounts on single and return tickets. They can get the same discounts for one travelling companion. Registered blind and partially sighted people without a Railcard can get the same discounts but only if they travel with a companion.

Underground or other transport systems may also offer concessions; ask at local offices.

Bus services

In England, from 1 April 2008, people aged 60 or over, and people with disabilities, are entitled to a free bus pass and a minimum concession of free off-peak travel on buses in every area of the country, whether using the bus locally or when visiting other parts of the country.

Local authorities may also offer discounted travel on other modes of transport, such as trams or rail, at their discretion. Where local authorities offer more generous schemes, they can make a charge, as long as a free pass providing the statutory minimum remains available as an option.

In Wales, people aged 60 and over, and people with disabilities, are entitled to free bus travel throughout Wales.

In Scotland, people aged 60 and over, and people with disabilities, are entitled to free bus travel throughout Scotland.

FOR MORE INFORMATION, contact your local authority (district or unitary council), or, in metropolitan areas, the Passenger Transport Executive (PTE).

Coach services

People who are 60 and over, and people who have a local authority concessionary travel pass because they are disabled, may be able to get coach fares at half price in England and Wales. Participation in this scheme is voluntary but National Express, the major provider, is a part of the scheme. The offer might not be available during some peak periods or on some tickets.

In Scotland the same rules apply as for bus concessions.

Taxicard schemes

Some local authorities operate taxicard schemes which provide reduced fares for disabled people. Contact your local authority to find out if it runs a scheme.

Airlines

Some airlines may have concessionary fares for pensioners. Ask at the airline or travel agent for details.

FOR MORE INFORMATION about help with the costs of travel, contact the Age Concern Information Line on 0800 00 99 66.

OTHER CONCESSIONS

People over a certain age or who are entitled to a State Pension may be able to receive concessions such as: reductions at leisure centres and swimming pools; lower admission prices to places of interest; and sometimes reduced fees for joining adult education classes. Most national museums now have free entry. Sometimes local businesses such as hairdressers may have special rates at certain times of the week. These concessions vary, so look out for any reductions that might apply to you.

Television

Television licences are free for households with a person aged 75 and over.

There are two other types of concession. People who are registered blind can obtain a 50 per cent reduction from the full licence fee. It is also possible to get specially adapted TV sound receivers and these do not need a licence to operate. Some people over the age of 60 who live in care homes or certain sheltered accommodation qualify for a concessionary £7.50 licence.

For more information, contact TV Licensing on 0870 241 6468 (www.tvlicensing.co.uk).

Digital Switchover Help Scheme The digital switchover will be taking place between 2008 and 2012, ITV region by ITV region. This means that once the transition is completed in your region, you will need to have digital equipment to continue watching television. Some people will receive support with installation and use of digital TV equipment.

The Help Scheme is available to people who are aged 75 or over, or registered blind or partially sighted, or entitled to Disability Living Allowance or Attendance Allowance (or equivalent). Help will be free for those who are eligible and who also receive Income Support, Jobseeker's Allowance or Pension Credit; other eligible people will have to pay a subsidised one-off fee of £40.

If you are eligible for help you will be sent details of the scheme before your area goes digital and you will need to respond to the letter.

For more information, see Age Concern Information Guide Digital Switchover: Questions and Answers,

191

which is available from the Age Concern Information Line on 0800 00 99 66. Or you can look at the Digital UK website (www.digitaluk.co.uk) or phone them on 0845 6505050 (lo-call rate).

Passports

Since 18 October 2004, British citizens born on or before 2 September 1929 have been eligible for free ten-year passports. These are renewable on expiry without charge. Those who are eligible and purchased a passport between 19 May 2004 and 18 October 2004 are able to apply for a refund by writing to their regional passport office.

FOR MORE INFORMATION, look on the Identity and Passport Service website (www.passport.gov.uk) or contact the Passport Adviceline on 0870 521 0410.

HELP FROM CHARITIES OR BENEVOLENT FUNDS

If you have checked that you are getting all the benefits you are entitled to and it is still hard to manage financially, you could try asking for help from charities or benevolent funds. Assistance may be available either as a lump sum or regular weekly payments. If you are receiving Pension Credit (see pages 50–75), all charitable payments made to you will be ignored.

Benevolent funds help people in particular circumstances – for example, these might be based on your occupation (or former occupation) or that of your partner; any health problems or disabilities you may have; or the area where you live. Others may help people who are members of trade unions or who have a particular religious belief.

FOR MORE INFORMATION, contact a local advice agency. There are also two national organisations – The Association of Charity Officers and Charity Search – that can help put people in contact with charities and benevolent funds. Their addresses are on page 206.

LEGAL FEES, WILLS AND FUNERALS

Help with legal costs and making wills

If you need help with a legal problem, you may be able to obtain this free from a local advice agency or you may be eligible for legal aid to help with the costs of a solicitor's fees. If you are on Pension Credit, Income Support or income-based Jobseeker's Allowance, or have a low income and little or no savings, you may be able to obtain help with legal advice and representation through the different Legal Aid schemes. This can include help with solicitors' fees for making a will, but in England and Wales you must be 70 or over or mentally or physically disabled in order to receive help. Community Legal Advice, run by the Legal Services Commission, can advise you whether you qualify for legal aid, and can provide free legal advice on some subjects if you qualify.

FOR MORE INFORMATION, contact the Age Concern Information Line on 0800 00 99 66 or Community Legal Advice on 0845 345 4345 (www.legalservices. gov.uk). The Scottish Legal Aid Board also publishes leaflets on Legal Aid. Its address is on page 210.

Help with Funeral Payments

This section describes the Funeral Payments available from the Social Fund which are part of the social

193

security system. For more details about arranging a funeral, including information about the duty of local and health authorities to pay for certain funerals, contact the Age Concern Information Line on 0800 00 99 66.

You may be able to receive a Social Fund Funeral Payment towards the cost of a funeral if you have good reason for taking responsibility for the expenses and you or your partner are receiving Pension Credit, Income Support, Housing Benefit, Council Tax Benefit, income-based Jobseeker's Allowance or Working Tax Credit where a disability or severe disability element is included in the award. Any savings you have will not be taken into account. However, as explained below, there are restrictions on who can receive a payment and limits on the amount of the payment, so it is very important to check what you are entitled to before making the arrangements.

To receive a payment you should be the partner of the person who has died, or someone else who it is reasonable to expect to take responsibility for arranging the funeral. The person who died must have been ordinarily resident in the UK and the funeral must normally take place in the UK, but in some circumstances it can take place elsewhere in a Member State of the European Union, Iceland, Liechtenstein, Norway or Switzerland.

Unless you are the partner of the person who has died, the decision-maker may decide, based on the nature and extent of your contact with the person who has died, that it was not reasonable for you to have taken responsibility for the funeral costs. The payment can cover necessary burial and cremation costs, certain necessary travel expenses and up to £700 for other funeral expenses.

Although your savings do not affect your entitlement to a Funeral Payment, if there is money available from the estate of the person who has died, or money from insurance policies or pre-paid funeral plans, this will be deducted from any award that would have been made.

To make a claim you will need form SF200 from Jobcentre Plus. You have to claim within three months of the funeral, but it is advisable to check what you are entitled to before arranging a funeral.

FOR MORE INFORMATION, contact the Age Concern Information Line on 0800 00 99 66 or see DWP leaflet D49 What To Do After a Death.

Further Information

This part of *Your Rights* gives details about local and national sources of help to contact for assistance and advice. In addition, there is information about obtaining Department for Work and Pensions (DWP) leaflets, Age Concern information, and other publications on benefits mentioned in the book. Also included is an index to help you find the information you require in this book and a summary of the main benefit rates.

DEPARTMENT FOR WORK AND PENSIONS

Much of the information in *Your Rights* covers State Pensions and benefits. The government department responsible is the Department for Work and Pensions (DWP). The rules for State Pensions and benefits and the levels of payment are set out in legislation – for example, each year regulations are agreed in Parliament setting out the annual increases to pensions and benefits.

In April 2008 the Pension Service and Disability and Carers Service were brought together as a single agency – the Pension, Disability and Carers Service. In the short term, however, as far as customers are concerned the services will continue to operate as before, with the same names and numbers, so they are described separately below and throughout this book.

The Pension Service is the part of the DWP responsible for State Pensions, Pension Credit and Winter Fuel Payments, and for providing information about other pension-related entitlements, including State Pension forecasts to help those of working age in planning for their future.

The Disability and Carers Service is responsible for Attendance Allowance, Disability Living Allowance and Carer's Allowance.

Jobcentre Plus deals with people of working age by administering benefits and providing advice and support about employment opportunities. It is also responsible for Social Fund payments (other than Winter Fuel Payments). Details of your local Jobcentre Plus office can be found in the phone book.

Problems with administration

If you have a problem with the administration of a benefit – for example if there is a delay in processing your claim – you can make your complaint to The Pension Service by phone, letter or email, or by using leaflet GL22 *Tell Us How to Improve our Service.* If you are still dissatisfied, get in touch with a local advice agency or your MP.

The Pension Service

The Pension Service delivers services and products through a network of pension centres across England, Scotland and Wales. The pension centres deal with customers by phone, post or email, and are supported by a local service which offers face-to-face contact. There is also a National Pension Centre and phone lines covering specific aspects of State Pensions and benefits.

To contact The Pension Service phone 0845 606 0265 8.00am–8.00pm weekdays (Textphone: 0845 606 0285) – this will connect you with the pension centre covering your area. Welsh language customers living in Wales should ring 0845 606 0275 (Textphone: 0845 606 0295). Staff there will provide information and answer queries about your State Pension and other pension-related entitlements. They can also tell you about local service, including details of information points in your area and home visits. You can find the postal or email address of your pension centre at www.thepension service. gov.uk /contact

National/International Pension Service addresses and phone lines People are encouraged to use the phone to contact The Pension Service, but if you prefer to write you can use the address below for State Pension

Forecasting, the National Pension Centre and the International Pension Centre.

The Pension Service
Tyneview Park
Whitley Road
Benton
Newcastle upon Tyne NE98 1BA

State Pension Forecasting Service
For a State Pension forecast, phone 0845 300 0168 (Textphone: 0845 300 0169). Forecasts can be obtained up to 30 days prior to reaching State Pension age (currently 60 for women born on or before 5 April 1950, 65 for men). At the time of writing, the systems are being updated to take into account the changes that are being introduced. So forecasts can only be made for those reaching State Pension age on or before 5 April 2010. The full service should be running by Autumn 2008.

Pensions Direct
Deals with changes of circumstances and enquiries for the people who have their pension paid direct into an account. Tel: 0845 301 3011, 8.00am–8.00pm weekdays. Textphone: 0845 301 3012.

International Pension Centre
For information about pensions and medical cover for those who live, or have previously lived, overseas. Tel: 0191 218 7777, 8.00am–8.00pm weekdays. Textphone: 0191 218 7280.

Pension Credit
To apply for Pension Credit by phone, or to get an application form, phone 0800 99 1234 (a free call), 8.00am–8.00pm weekdays, 9.00am–1.00pm Saturdays. Textphone: 0800 169 0133.

Disability and Carers Service
Disability Contact and Processing Unit
Warbreck House
Warbreck Hill Road
Blackpool FY2 0YE
Tel: 0845 7123456, 7.30am–6.30pm weekdays.
Textphone: 0845 7224433 (you can also use the RNID
Typetalk service).

The Disability and Carers Service administers Disability
Living Allowance and Attendance Allowance, although
initial claims are normally dealt with at the regionally
based Disability Benefit Centres.

Carer's Allowance Unit
Palatine House
Lancaster Road
Preston
Lancashire PR1 1HB
Tel: 01253 856 123, 8.15am–5.00pm
Mondays–Thursdays, 8.15am–4.30pm Fridays
Textphone: 01772 899 489

Benefit Enquiry Line for people with disabilities and carers
For advice and information about disability benefits,
phone 0800 88 22 00 (a free call), 8.30am–6.30pm
weekdays, 9.00am–1.00pm Saturdays. Textphone: 0800
24 33 55 (you can also use the RNID Typetalk service).

Staff can arrange for help with completing forms over
the phone for benefits such as Attendance Allowance and
Disability Living Allowance.

DWP/Pension Service websites

If you have access to the internet, you can obtain leaflets, publications and other information from the websites. You can also download claim forms for many benefits.

Websites: www.dwp.gov.uk,
www.thepensionservice.gov.uk and www.direct.gov.uk

AGE CONCERN INFORMATION LINE

The Age Concern Information Line (ACIL) is a service for older people, their relatives and friends and those who care for and work with them. ACIL provides free written information on a wide range of subjects affecting older people, including money and benefits, finding and paying for care, housing issues, health services and healthy living, consumer issues, common legal questions for older people and age discrimination and employment.

ACIL can be contacted by calling 0800 00 99 66 (8am–7pm, days a week) or by writing to:

Age Concern
Freepost (SWB 30375)
Ashburton
Devon TQ13 7ZZ

All of Age Concern's range of information can also be viewed and downloaded for free from our website (www.ageconcern.org.uk).

Materials available include information guides that provide a general introduction to these subjects and detailed factsheets for professionals and individuals who have a specific enquiry or problem. To receive a free email update when new and updated Age Concern information products are published, send your email contact details to factsheet.subscriptions@ace.org.uk

Where possible Age Concern's information is applicable across the UK. There are differences in the law between England, Northern Ireland, Scotland and Wales, however, and for some subjects enquirers from these nations may be provided with different versions of materials or signposted to their national office.

LOCAL SOURCES OF HELP

Age Concern

Most areas have a local Age Concern which provides services and advice. You can find the address from the phone book, library or Citizens Advice, or you can write to the appropriate national Age Concern (addresses on page 222) or call the Age Concern Information Line (Freephone 0800 00 99 66) for the address of the nearest local Age Concern to you.

Citizens Advice

The local offices provide advice and information on all kinds of subjects, including benefits, housing and consumer problems. You can find out where your nearest Citizens Advice is from the phone book or at your local library. The Citizens Advice website (www.adviceguide. org.uk) offers advice on a range of issues such as employment, consumer advice and benefits.

Law centre

There may be a law centre giving free legal advice in your area. Check in the phone book or at a Citizens Advice, or contact Community Legal Advice on 0845 345 4345. Community Legal Advice (which is funded by the Legal Services Commission) also offers information about your rights and how to obtain legal advice, and its website (www.clsdirect.org.uk) gives useful legal information. The Law Centres Federation website (www.lawcentres.org.uk) may also be of interest.

Local authority/council

In England the structure of local government depends on whether you live in a county, or in a metropolitan or London borough, or a unitary authority. All areas in Scotland and Wales have a unitary authority. In England, if you live in a county, the district council will deal with Housing Benefit, Council Tax Benefit and other matters to do with the Council Tax. You will need to contact the county council about social services. In a metropolitan or London borough, or unitary authority, there will be just one authority that will deal with the Council Tax, Housing Benefit and social services. Some authorities have welfare rights workers to advise on benefits. You will find the address of your local authority in the phone book under the name of your county, unitary authority, metropolitan or London borough, or ask at your local library.

Local councillor

A councillor for your area may be able to help with problems with the local authority. You can get the names of the councillors for your 'ward' from the town hall, library or Citizens Advice.

Local Government Ombudsman

If you feel you have suffered because of maladministration in the way the local authority has dealt with your case, you can make a complaint to the Local Government Ombudsman (or the Scottish Public Services Ombudsman or the Public Services Ombudsman for Wales). You can do this direct or through your local councillor. Ask a local advice agency or councillor for further information or look at the website at www.lgo.org.uk (www.spso.org.uk in Scotland or www.ombudsman-wales.org.uk in Wales).

Member of Parliament (MP)

Your MP may be able to help with problems involving government departments. If you do not know who your MP is, ask at the town hall, library or Citizens Advice or ring the House of Commons Information Office on 020 7219 4272. Most MPs hold regular surgeries locally; or you can write to your MP at the House of Commons, London SW1A 0AA. For a complaint about unfair treatment by a government department (for example a delay with a benefit claim), ask the MP to refer your complaint to the Parliamentary Ombudsman.

In Scotland you can contact Members of the Scottish Parliament at Scottish Parliament, Edinburgh EH99 1SP or ring 0131 348 5000.

In Wales you can contact Assembly Members at the National Assembly for Wales, Cardiff Bay, Cardiff CF99 1NA or ring the Public Information and Education Team on 0845 010 5500 (local rate).

Trade union

If you were a member of a trade union before retirement, it may be worth contacting your local branch, particularly for problems over a pension from work.

Welfare rights and money advice centres

There may be an independent welfare rights or money advice centre locally. Money advice centres generally deal with debt problems and may only accept referrals from other agencies.

NATIONAL SOURCES OF INFORMATION

The national organisations listed below may be able to help or put you in touch with a source of advice.

Association of Charity Officers
Five Ways
57–59 Hatfield Road
Potters Bar
Hertfordshire EN6 1HS
Tel: 01707 651777, weekdays 10.00am–4.00pm
Website: www.aco.uk.net
Provides information about charities that make grants to individuals in need.

Carers UK
32–36 Loman Street
London SE1 0EE
Tel: 020 7922 8000
CarersLine: 0808 808 7777, Wednesdays–Thursdays
10.00am–12.00pm and 2.00pm–4.00pm
Website: www.carersuk.org
Provides general advice and help for all carers.

Charity Search
25 Portview Road
Avonmouth
Bristol BS11 9LD
Tel: 0117 982 4060, Mondays–Thursdays
9.30am–2.30pm
Helps link older people with charities that may provide grants to individuals. Applications in writing are preferred.

Counsel and Care
Twyman House
16 Bonny Street
London NW1 9PG
Advice line (local rate call): 0845 300 7585, weekdays
10.00am–4.00pm, except Wednesdays 10.00am-1.00pm
Website: www.counselandcare.org.uk
*Advises on obtaining and paying for care in a care home
and a range of community care issues.*

Disability Alliance
Universal House
88–94 Wentworth Street
London E1 7SA
Tel: 020 7247 8776
Website: www.disabilityalliance.org
Produces Disability Rights Handbook *(see page 211)
and other publications, and gives advice on social
security benefits for disabled people.*

Disabled Persons Railcard Office
PO Box 163
Newcastle upon Tyne NE12 8WX
Application helpline: 0845 605 0525
Textphone: 0845 601 0132
Website: www.disabledpersons-railcard.co.uk
For a railcard offering concessionary fares.

EAGA Partnership Ltd
Freephone: 0800 316 2808 (England)
Freephone: 0800 316 2815 (Wales)
Website: www.eaga.co.uk
*Administers the Warm Front grants in England and
Home Energy Efficiency Scheme in Wales (described on
pages 169–171).*

Foundations
Bleaklow House
Howard Town Mill
Glossop SK13 8HT
Tel: 01457 891909
Website: www.foundations.uk.com
The national co-ordinating body for Home Improvement Agencies in England.

HM Revenue & Customs National Insurance Contributions Office (NICO)
Benton Park View
Newcastle upon Tyne NE98 1ZZ
Tel: 0845 302 1479
Website: www.hmrc.gov.uk/nic
For information about NI contributions and records and Statutory Sick Pay. HM Revenue & Customs (formerly the Inland Revenue) is also responsible for tax credits. To find details of offices and HMRC Tax Enquiry Centres, look in the phone book under 'Inland Revenue' or 'HM Revenue & Customs'.

Independent Living Funds
PO Box 7525
Nottingham NG2 4ZT
Tel: 0845 601 8815
Website: www.ilf.org.uk
For information and a user guide about the ILF.

Motability
City Gate House
22 Southwark Bridge Road
London SE1 9HB
Tel: 0845 456 4566
Website: www.motability.co.uk

The Motability Scheme offers help to people in receipt of either the higher rate of the mobility component of Disability Living Allowance or the War Pensioners' Mobility Supplement. Offers the chance to buy or lease a car at an affordable price. May also be able to offer financial help towards the cost of a suitable car, adaptations, driving lessons or a wheelchair-accessible vehicle.

The Pensions Advisory Service (TPAS)
11 Belgrave Road
London SW1V 1RB
Helpline: 0845 601 2923
Website: www.opas.org.uk
Offers help and advice about pensions. Will also help anyone with a problem with their occupational or personal pension arrangement.

Royal National Institute of Blind People (RNIB)
105 Judd Street
London WC1H 9NE
Tel: 020 7388 1266
Helpline: 0845 766 9999
Website: www.rnib.org.uk
Offers advice and information on social security and other issues for blind and partially sighted people.

Royal National Institute for Deaf People (RNID)
RNID Information Line
19–23 Featherstone Street
London EC1Y 8SL
Tel: 020 7296 8000
Freephone Helpline: 0808 808 0123
Freephone Textphone: 0808 808 9000
Website: www.rnid.org.uk
Provides information for deaf and hard of hearing people.

209

Scottish Legal Aid Board (SLAB)

44 Drumsheugh Gardens
Edinburgh EH3 7SW
Tel: 0131 226 7061
Legal Aid Helpline: 0845 122 8686
Website: www.slab.org.uk
Publishes leaflets about legal aid for people in Scotland.

Service Personnel and Veterans Agency

Norcross
Thornton Cleveleys
Lancashire FY5 3WP
Veterans Helpline: 0800 169 2277 (free call),
Mondays–Thursdays 8.15am–5.15pm, Fridays
8.15am–4.30pm
Textphone: 0800 169 3458
Website: www.veteransagency.mod.uk
The Service Personnel and Veterans Agency is
responsible for the War Pensions Scheme and is also the
point of contact within the Ministry of Defence for
information and advice on issues of concern to veterans
and their families.

> *For information about national organisations in*
> *Scotland, Wales and Northern Ireland, contact the*
> *appropriate national Age Concern (addresses on*
> *page 222).*

FURTHER READING

Government leaflets

As well as the leaflets mentioned in *Your Rights,* there is
a catalogue of all the DWP leaflets produced (Cat1) on
the Department for Work and Pensions website
(www.dwp.gov.uk). The leaflets should be available from
your local Jobcentre Plus office or pension centre, and

they are sometimes in libraries, post offices or Citizens Advice offices. Many are also available on the internet at www.dwp.gov.uk (or www.thepensionservice.gov.uk).

HM Revenue & Customs (formerly the Inland Revenue) deals with issues relating to NI contributions. Leaflets on contributions can be obtained from tax offices or on the HMRC website (www.hmrc.gov.uk).

Leaflets on help with health costs are available from the Department of Health, PO Box 777, London SE1 6XH, on the internet at www.doh.gov.uk or by ringing the Health Literature Line on 08701 555 455.

Other publications

For detailed information on services and benefits for disabled people, you may wish to get the *Disability Rights Handbook 2008/09*, £21 (£14.50 for individuals receiving any State benefits), available from the Disability Alliance, Universal House, 88–94 Wentworth Street, London E1 7SA. Tel: 020 7247 8776. Website: www.disabilityalliance.org

For detailed information on all benefits, with reference to the relevant government legislation, you may wish to refer to the *Welfare Benefits and Tax Credits Handbook 2008/09*, £36 plus £3.99 post and packing (£8.50 post free for individual benefit claimants), which is available from the Child Poverty Action Group (CPAG), 94 White Lion Street, London N1 9PF. Tel: 020 7837 7979. Website: www.cpag.org.uk This book covers both means-tested and non-means-tested benefits.

These books may also be available for reference at your local library.

BENEFIT RATES APRIL 2008/09

Some of the main weekly benefit rates are listed below for quick reference:

State Pensions and disability benefits
Attendance Allowance

higher rate	£67.00
lower rate	£44.85

Disability Living Allowance
care component

highest rate	£67.00
middle rate	£44.85
lowest rate	£17.75

mobility component

higher rate	£46.75
lower rate	£17.75

Carer's Allowance	£50.55
Incapacity Benefit (long-term rate)	£84.50
Severe Disablement Allowance (basic rate)	£51.05

State Pension

basic rate	£90.70
wife on husband's contributions	£54.35
couple on husband's contributions	£145.05

Income-related benefits

Housing Benefit/Council Tax Benefit standard applicable amounts for people aged 65 or over

single person	£143.80
couple	£215.50

Pension Credit standard appropriate amounts and Housing Benefit/Council Tax Benefit applicable amounts for people aged 60–64

single person	£124.05
couple	£189.35

Pension Credit maximum savings credit

single person	£19.71
couple	£26.13

Premiums/additions

severe disability	£50.35
carer	£27.75

KEEPING UP TO DATE

This edition of *Your Rights* is based on the information available in March 2008. The benefit levels will normally apply until the first week in April 2009. A new edition of the book will be published next year to cover the period from April 2009 to April 2010. However, sometimes changes are made during the course of a year.

If you would like us to inform you of any major changes introduced before April 2009, please cut off this page and return it to the address below.

Write in with your details if you do not want to cut up the book.

Dear Age Concern

Please send me details about any major changes introduced before April 2009

Name (block letters)

_____

Signature

_____

Address

_____

_____

Postcode

_____

Please return to:

Age Concern (YR Update)
FREEPOST (SWB 30375)
Ashburton
Devon TQ13 7ZZ

INDEX

Age Concern is the UK's largest organisation working for and with older people to enable them to make more of life. A federation of over 400 independent charities that share the same name, values and standards, we believe that later life should be fulfilling, enjoyable and productive.

Age Concern publishes a wide range of bestselling books that help thousands of people each year. Our books provide practical, trusted advice on a range of subjects, from finance and retirement planning to health and surfing the web. Whether you are acting as a carer or want to know more about your rights to healthcare or employment, we have something for everyone.

To find out more, to order a free catalogue or to buy a book please call our hotline on 0870 44 22 120 or visit the website at www.ageconcern.org.uk/bookshop. You can also buy our books from all good bookshops.

Age Concern England
1268 London Road
London, SW16 4ER
Tel: 020 8765 7200
www.ageconcern.org.uk

Age Concern Scotland
Causewayside House
160 Causewayside
Edinburgh, EH9 1PR
Tel: 0845 833 0200
www.ageconcernscotland.
org.uk

Age Concern Cymru
Ty John Pathy
Units 13 and 14 Neptune Court
Vanguard Way
Cardiff, CF24 5PJ
Tel: 029 2043 1555
www.accymru.org.uk

Age Concern Northern Ireland
3 Lower Crescent
Belfast, BT7 1NR
Tel: 028 9024 5729
www.ageconcernni.org

Age Concern Information: we produce a range of comprehensive information guides designed to answer many of the questions that older people – or those advising them – may have. These free guides cover issues such as housing, care homes, pensions, benefits, health, community care, leisure and education, and can be obtained by calling our free information line on 0800 00 99 66 or by downloading them from the website (www.ageconcern.org.uk).

MORE GREAT BOOKS FROM AGE CONCERN

Our new *We've made it easy* series has been specially designed to help you make sense of your money. Concise and easy-to-read, with plenty of helpful case studies, this series make it easier than ever for you to take control of your finances and make your money work harder for you.

Pay less tax
Second edition (published May 08)

Many people don't realise that millions of pounds are lost each year because of inaccurate tax payments – and those who do realise often don't know what to do about it. *Pay less tax*, written by Paul Lewis, presenter of Radio 4's 'Money Box', will help you make sense of all things tax related. It explains income tax, tax allowances, your tax code, self-employment, inheritance tax, and much more. If you've ever felt confused by taxation, then this is the book you need.

£5.99 + postage and packing   978-0-86242-435-0

Beat the banks

Beat the banks is your no-nonsense guide to saving, investing and getting the most from your money. It explains how you could be missing out on valuable income by not shopping around for the best deals. *Beat the banks* shows how easy it can be to seek out more rewarding places to save your money and make it grow. It also demystifies investments and explains those financial terms you may have heard of but never properly understood.

£5.99 + postage and packing   978-0-86242-431-2